Mediterranean Diet for Beginners 2019-2020

The Complete Guide - 21-Day Diet Meal Plan - Lose Up to 20 Pounds in 3 Weeks

By Susan Skylar

Table of Content

Introduction

The food and culture are interwoven inseparably. We learn what good food is from the elders, who have in turn learned the same thing themselves from the previous generation. In this way, national recipes and tastes are both acquired and inherited, becoming an integral part of the cultural identity, something that we carry within us no matter where we end up living. Some families go so far as to have their own twists and tweaks of the traditional dishes that are jealously guarded against all foreigners. Through the wonders of modern mobility, cultures combine like never before and different dishes meld, creating something completely unique and endemic.

The Western countries are a wonderful example of national cuisines from all over the world coming together in a single crock pot. Seeing a string of national restaurants right in the middle of a modern metropolis such as Munich is by now a completely ordinary sight, but the fact that one can order and simultaneously eat authentic kebabs and gyros is simply amazing. No matter how different they are, these various dishes still share a common ancestry, one which has been pinpointed as originating from the area roughly surrounding the Mediterranean Sea.

This so-called "Mediterranean diet" involves diets found in countries such as Croatia, Italy, and Greece and is actually representative of how the same dishes can be prepared differently using the same or similar ingredients.

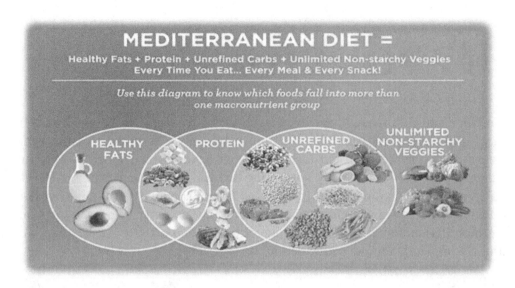

Abundant in olive oil, fresh fruits, cheese, and yogurt, the Mediterranean diet has been found to favorably affect the blood pressure, shielding the cardiovascular system from damage and degeneration. Another favorable factor in this diet is that it inherently eschews alcohol and eggs, with red meat being replaced by poultry and fish. Identified in the 1970s as such, the Mediterranean diet eventually found its way on the UNESCO Cultural Heritage list. Medical examination of data regarding large swathes of people who spent their lives on the Mediterranean diet also supports the common-sense conclusion that it is indeed a healthful way of living.

Both cancer and coronary disease risk factors are eliminated through the faithful application of the Mediterranean diet. The same applies to Alzheimer's and Parkinson's disease, which are nothing other than degenerative maladies affecting the brain. Studies differ slightly in how effective this diet is in reducing the risk, but the meta-studies calculate the median as being 9%. A 2010 study of available data showed that the Mediterranean diet reduces the risk of other chronic diseases as well, such as atherosclerosis and arthritis. Another study in 2011 conclusively proved that this diet also lowers the blood sugar, triglycerides, and blood pressure.

When it comes to type-2 diabetes, the Mediterranean diet can also help. Since this affliction is positively correlated to body weight and blood pressure, both of which this diet helps manage, the abundance of filling fruits, vegetables and olive oil found in the Mediterranean diet help lower the risk of sudden onsets of hunger, cravings, and binges. In this way, the Mediterranean diet can be said to be completely sustainable, as it contains all the basic nutrients in sufficient quantities delivered in the most natural and wholesome way.

By reducing your risk of developing heart disease or cancer with the Mediterranean diet, you're reducing your risk of death at any age by 20%. Protecting against type 2 diabetes. A Mediterranean diet is rich in fiber which digests slowly, prevents huge swings in blood sugar, and can help you maintain a healthy weight.

There is still a lot of mysteries related to diet and how any single food affects our bodies. It is quite a life's paradox that we continue to eat and we are obliged to eat without necessarily knowing what is it we're eating or why we feel compelled to eat that particular food. This is where the wisdom of ancestors proves indispensable – by observing, following and respecting the dietary traditions of our people, we can conclusively prove to ourselves which of the diets available to us is the healthiest.

When faced with the abundance of culinary choices, all we have to do is turn to the food that we personally find to be the most fulfilling.

The Mediterranean diet traditionally includes fruits, vegetables, pasta, and rice. For example, residents of Greece eat very little red meat and an average of nine servings a day of antioxidant-rich fruits and vegetables. Nuts are another part of a healthy Mediterranean diet.

Chapter 1 – The Complete Mediterranean Diet 101

What is the Mediterranean Diet?

The Mediterranean diet refers to the traditional eating habits and lifestyles of people living around the Mediterranean Sea – Italy, Spain, France, Greece, and some North African countries. The Mediterranean diet has become very popular in recent times, as people from these regions have better health and suffer from fewer ailments, such as cancer and cardiovascular issues. Food plays a key role in this.

Research has uncovered the many benefits of this diet. According to the results of a 2013 study, many overweight and diabetic patients showed a surprising improvement in their cardiovascular health after eating the Mediterranean diet for 5 years. The study was conducted among 7000 people in Spain. There was a marked 30% reduction in cardiovascular disease in this high-risk group.

The report took the world by storm after the New England Journal of Medicine published the findings. Several studies have indicated its many health benefits – the Mediterranean diet may stabilize the level of blood sugar, prevent Alzheimer's disease, reduce the risk of heart disease and stroke, improve brain health, ease anxiety and depression, promote weight loss, and even lower the risk of certain types of cancer.

The diet differs from country to country, and even within the regions of these countries because of cultural, ethnic, agricultural, religious, and economic differences. So there is no one standard Mediterranean diet. However, there are several common factors.

The Mediterranean Diet Pyramid

The Med diet food pyramid is a nutrition guide to help people eat the right foods in the correct quantities and the prescribed frequency as per the traditional eating habits of people from the Mediterranean coast countries.

The pyramid was developed by the World Health Organization, Harvard School of Public Health, and the old ways Preservation Trust in 1993.

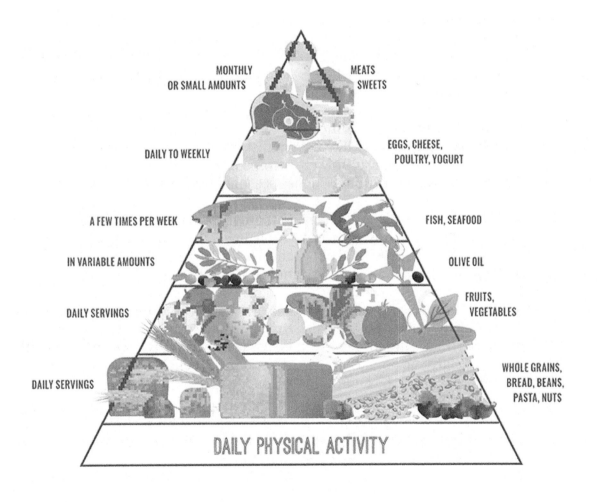

There are 6 food layers in the pyramid with physical activity at the base, which is an important element to maintain a healthy life.

Just above it is the first food layer, consisting of whole grains, breads, beans, pasta, and nuts. It is the strongest layer having foods that are recommended by the Mediterranean diet. Next comes fruits and vegetables. As you move up the pyramid, you will find foods that must be eaten less and less, with the topmost layer consisting of foods that should be avoided or restricted.

The Mediterranean diet food pyramid is easy to understand. It provides an easy way to follow the eating plan.

The Food Layers

1. **Whole Grains, Breads, Beans** – The lowest and the widest layer with foods that are strongly recommended. Your meals should be made of mostly these items. Eat whole-wheat bread, whole-wheat pita, whole-grain roll and bun, whole-grain cereal, whole-wheat pasta, and brown rice. 4 to 6 servings a day will give you plenty of nutrition.

2. **Fruits, Vegetables** – Almost as important as the lowest layer. Eat non-starchy vegetables daily like asparagus, broccoli, beets, tomatoes, carrots, cucumber, cabbage, cauliflower, turnips 4 to 8 servings daily. Take 2 to 4 servings of fruits every day. Choose seasonal fresh fruits.

3. **Olive oil** – Cook your meals preferably in extra-virgin olive oil. Daily consumption. Healthy for the body, it lowers the low-density lipoprotein cholesterol (LDL) and total cholesterol level. Up to 2 tablespoons of olive oil is allowed. The diet also allows canola oil.

4. **Fish** – Now we come to the food layers that have to be consumed weekly and not daily. You can have fish 2 to 3 times a week. Best is fatty sea fish like tuna, herring, salmon, and sardines. Sea fish will give you heart-healthy omega-3 fatty acids and plenty of proteins. Shellfish, including mussels, oysters, shrimp, and clams are also good.

5. **Poultry, cheese, yogurt** – The diet should include cheese, yogurt, eggs, chicken, and other poultry products, but in moderation. Maximum 2-3 times in a week. Low-fat dairy is best. Soy milk, cheese, or yogurt is better.

6. **Meats, sweets** – This is the topmost layer consisting of foods that are best avoided. You can have them once or twice in a month max. Remember, the Mediterranean diet is plant-based. There is very little room for meat, especially red meat. If you cannot live without it, then take red meat in small

portions. Choose lean cuts. Have sweets only to celebrate. For instance, you can have a couple of sweets after following the diet for a month.

Recommended Foods

For example, most people living in the region eat a diet rich in whole grains, vegetables, fruits, nuts, seeds, fish, fats, and legumes. It is not a restrictive diet like the many low-fat eating plans. Actually, fat is encouraged, but only from healthy sources, such as polyunsaturated fat (omega-3 fatty acids) that you will get from fish and monounsaturated fat from olive oil.

It is strongly plant-based, but not exclusively vegetarian. The diet recommends limiting the intake of saturated fats and trans fats that you get from red meat and processed foods. You must also limit the intake of dairy products.

- **Fruits and vegetables** – Eat daily. Try to have 7-10 servings every day. Meals are strongly based on plant-based foods. Eat fresh fruits and vegetables. Pick from seasonal varieties.

- **Whole grains** – Eat whole-grain cereal, bread, and pasta. All parts of whole grains – the germ, bran, and the endosperm provide healthy nutrients. These nutrients are lost when the grain is refined into white flour.

- **Healthy fats only** – Avoid butter for cooking. Switch to olive oil. Dip your bread in flavored olive oil instead of applying margarine or butter on bread. Trans fats and saturated fats can cause heart disease.

- **Fish** – Fish is encouraged. Eat fatty fish like herring, mackerel, albacore tuna, sardines, lake trout, and salmon. Fatty fish will give you plenty of healthy omega-3 fatty acids that reduce inflammations. Omega-3 fatty acids also reduced blood clotting, decreased triglycerides, and improves heart health. Eat fresh seafood two times a week. Avoid deep-fried fish. Choose grilled fish.

- **Legumes** – Provides the body with minerals, protein, complex carbohydrates, polyunsaturated fatty acids, and fiber. Eat daily.

- **Dairy and poultry** – You can eat eggs, milk products, and chicken throughout the week, but with moderation. Restrict cheese. Go for plain or low-fat Greek yogurt instead of cheese.

- **Nuts and seeds** – 3 or more servings every week. Eat a variety of nuts, seeds, and beans. Walnuts and almonds are all allowed.

- **Red meat** – The Mediterranean diet is not meat-based. You can still have red meat, but only once or twice a week max. If you love red meat, then make sure that it is lean. Take small portions only. Avoid processed meats like salami, sausage, and bologna.

- **Olive Oil** – The key source of fat. Olive oil will give you monounsaturated fat that lowers the LDL or low-density lipoprotein cholesterol and total cholesterol level. Seeds and nuts will also provide you monounsaturated fat. You can also have canola oil but no cream, butter, mayonnaise, or margarine. Take up to 4 tablespoons of olive oil a day. For best results, only take extra-virgin olive oil.

- **Wine** – Red wine is allowed, but with moderation. Don't take more than a glass of red wine daily. Best take only 3-4 days a week.

- **Desserts** – Say no to ice cream, sweets, pies, and chocolate cake. Fresh fruits are good.

Main Components –

- Focus on natural foods – Avoid processed foods as much as you can
- Be flexible – Plan to have a variety of foods
- Consume fruits, vegetables, healthy fats, and whole grains daily
- Have weekly plans for poultry, fish, eggs, and beans
- Take dairy products moderately
- Limit red meat intake
- Take water instead of soda. Only take wine when you are having a meal.

Foods in the Traditional Mediterranean Diet

Whole Grains	Vegetables	Fruits	Protein	Dairy	Others

Brown rice	Artichokes	Apples	Almonds	Low/non-fat plain or Greek yogurt	Bay leaf
Oats	Arugula	Apricots	Walnuts	Manchego cheese	Basil
Bulgur	Beats	Avocados	Pistachios	Brie cheese	Olive oil
Barley	Broccoli	Figs	Cannellini Beans	Ricotta cheese	Red wine
Farrow	Cucumbers	Olives	Chickpeas	Parmesan cheese	Mint
Wheat berries	Eggplant	Strawberries	Kidney beans	Feta cheese	Pepper
Pasta	Onions	Tomatoes	Salmon		cumin
Whole grain bread	Spinach	Melons	Tuna		Garlic
Couscous	Potatoes	Grapes	Eggs		Anise spice

Foods Allowed

You should consume plenty of fruits, vegetables, nuts, seeds, beans, whole grains, herbs, and legumes. Olive oil and canola oil are both allowed.

Eat Moderately

Fish, seafood, chicken, eggs, low-fat cheese, and yogurt.

Restricted Foods

This list includes refined grains like white rice, white bread, sweets, baked products, and soda. Also, restrict processed meats and red meat. Watch out for high-fat dairy products like butter and ice cream and trans-fats in margarine and processed foods.

Med Diet Serving Sizes

Food Groups and Daily/Weekly Servings	Serving Sizes
Non-starchy vegetables – **4 to 8 servings**	1 serving is ½ cup of cooked vegetables or 1 cup of raw vegetables Asparagus, artichoke, broccoli, beets, Brussels sprouts, cabbage, celery, cauliflower, carrots, eggplant, tomatoes, cucumber, onion, zucchini, turnips, mushrooms, and salad greens and. Note: Peas, corn, and potatoes are starchy vegetables.
Fruits – **2 to 4 servings**	One serving is a small fruit or ½ cup juice or ¼ cup dried fruit Eat fresh fruits for their nutrients and fiber. You can also have canned fruits with their juice and frozen fruits without added sugar.
Legumes, Nuts, Seeds – **2 to 4 servings**	Legumes – 1 serving is ½ cup cooked kidney, pinto, garbanzo, soy, navy beans, lentils, or split peas, or ¼ cup fat-free beans. Nuts and Seeds – 1 serving is 2 tablespoons of sesame or sunflower seeds, 1 tablespoon peanut butter, 7-8 pecans or walnuts, 12-15 almonds, 20 peanuts. Take 1-2 servings of nuts or seeds and 1-2 servings of legumes. Legumes will give you minerals, fiber, and protein, whole nuts provide unsaturated fat without increasing your LDL cholesterol levels.
Low-Fat Dairy – **2 to 3 servings**	1 serving is 1 cup of skim milk, non-fat yogurt, or 1 oz. low-fat cheese Replace dairy products with soy yogurt, calcium-rich soy milk, or soy cheese. You need a vitamin D and calcium supplement if you are taking less than 2 servings daily.
Fish – **2 to 3 times a week**	One serving is 3 ounces Bake, sauté, roast, broil, poach, or grill. It is best to eat fatty fish, such as sardines, herring, salmon, or mackerel. Fish will provide you omega-3 fats, which offers many health benefits.
Poultry – **1 to 3 times a week**	One serving is 3 ounces Sauté, bake, grill, or stir fry the poultry. Eat without the skin.

Whole grains, starchy vegetables – **4 to 6 servings**	One serving is 1 ounce of – ½ cup sweet potatoes, potatoes, corn, or peas 1 slice of whole-wheat bread 1 small whole-grain roll ½ large whole-grain bun 6 whole-grain crackers 6-inch whole wheat pita ½ cup cooked brown rice, whole-wheat pasta, or barley ½ cup whole-grain cereal (cracked wheat, oatmeal, quinoa) Whole grains provide fiber and keep the stomach full, promoting weight loss.
Healthy fats – **4 to 6 servings**	One serving is – 1 tablespoon of regular salad dressing 2 tablespoons of light salad dressing 2 teaspoons light margarine 1 teaspoon canola or olive oil 1 teaspoon regular mayonnaise 1/8 avocado 5 olives These are mostly unsaturated fats, so your LDL cholesterol levels won't increase.
Alcohol	Men – Max 2 drinks a day. Women – Max 1 drink a day. 1 drink = 4 ounces of wine, 12-ounce beer, or 1-1/2-ounces liquor (vodka, whiskey, brandy, etc.). Avoid alcohol if you have high triglycerides or high BP.

The Med Lifestyle

Not just the food, but the correct lifestyle is also equally important. This includes both getting adequate exercise and making social connections.

Physical Activity – It is at the base of the food pyramid, even lower than the first and most important food layer – getting adequate physical activity is essential.

This includes exercising regularly, swimming, biking, running, and playing an active sport. However, there are other ways as well to maintain good health.

You will find many from the Mediterranean region not going to the gym. But, they are not inactive. Many are into a lot of manual labor. They will walk to their workplace, to the bakery, or the farmer's market. They walk to their friend's home. Even a daily walk and moderate exercise will help. Natural movements are good. Avoid the escalator. Take the stairs instead.

How much exercising is good? Working out is always good for health. You don't have to lift weights, though. 10-15 minutes on the treadmill and gym bike 5 days a week should be good. Half an hour of moderate-intensity activity will do. Nothing better if you can also do a few muscle-strengthening activities twice a week. You can also try walking 200 minutes a week or even gardening for an hour 4-5 times a week.

Cook at Home – Home cooked food is always healthier than eating out. For example, restaurant cooked pasta will have higher portions of sodium. Again, you can have one portion of whole-grain spaghetti with tomato sauce and spinach instead of the heavy cream sauce. You can control the ingredients by preparing the meals at home. Home cooked meals have lots of minerals, vitamins, and fiber, and are lower in added sugar, sodium, and saturated fat.

Eat Together – The mealtime should be a social experience. Eating together with friends or family is a great stress buster. It will boost your mood, which will have a positive impact on your physical health. Plus, it will prevent you from overeating too. You will often find the Mediterranean people eating together in a garden.

Switch the TV off and enjoy your meal. Monitor what the kids are eating. If you live alone, invite a co-worker, neighbor, or friend. You can even invite someone and prepare meals together.

Laugh Often – Have you heard of the popular saying, "Laughter is the best medicine"? This is true in the Mediterranean culture. Many are individuals with a big personality. Their conversations are full of humor. They love to tell stories. Enjoy life and keep a positive attitude/

Live a Simple Life – Consider food, for example. You won't find them buying too much of anything. The idea of buying any ingredient in bulk is foreign to them. They buy fresh, focusing on daily needs. And of course, fresh food is always best.

<u>Enjoy Every Bite</u> – Slow down and enjoy each bite. Many will eat for survival. But in the Mediterranean belt, they love their food. They enjoy it. Don't eat on the go. Sit down and have a proper meal.

Health Benefits of the Med Diet

1. **Heart disease and stroke** – The Mediterranean diet recommends limited eating of processed foods, red meat, and refined breads, which contributes towards a lower risk of heart ailments and stroke. A study carried out over 12 years among 25,000 women found that women eating this diet were able to reduce their risk of heart disease by 25%.

   The PREDIMED (1) study was carried out amongst men and women with a high-risk of cardiovascular disease and type-2 diabetes in Spain. After 5 years of research, it was discovered that those who had a calorie-unrestricted Mediterranean diet had a 30% lower risk of heart issues.

2. **Alzheimer's** – Research also suggests that the diet can improve blood sugar levels, cholesterol, and blood vessel health, which in turn may lower the risk of dementia and Alzheimer's disease. A 2018 study (2) scanned the brains of 70 people for dementia and monitored their food habits. After 2 years, it was observed that those on the Mediterranean diet had fewer protein plaques or beta-amyloid deposits than others, and thus a lower risk of Alzheimer's.

   Other studies have also revealed that the Mediterranean diet may also prevent the decline of thinking skills and memory with age as there is an increased supply of oxygen and nutrients to the brain.

   The diet is packed with antioxidants, such as olive oil and nuts, which may delay mental decline. A link between consuming fish and lower risk of Alzheimer's has also been found.

3. **Diabetes** – The diet with healthy carbs and whole grains offers big benefits like stabilizing the blood sugar level. Complex whole grain carbs like wheat berries, buckwheat, and quinoa improves overall energy and keeps the sugar level even in your blood. Research on more than 400 people between the age of 55 and 80 years have revealed that the Mediterranean diet can lower (3) the risk of type-2 diabetes by 52%. This study was carried out over 4 years.

4. **Parkinson's disease** – The diet is rich in antioxidants, which may prevent oxidative stress or cell damage, thus reducing the risk of Parkinson's disease by as much as 50%.

5. **Weight loss** – The Mediterranean diet gives you plenty of fiber that will make you feel satiated. You won't overeat as a result. The diet improves metabolism and promotes healthy weight loss. Just remember to focus on consuming fibrous vegetables, fruits, beans, and legumes instead of simple carbohydrates. This is a safe and sustainable way to lose weight as almost nothing is denied in the overall meal plan. The U.S. News & World Report ranked Mediterranean diet #1 in the 'Best Overall Diet' category for 2019.

6. **Cancer** – The diet has also been linked to a lower risk of certain types of cancer. Researchers looked at the findings of 83 studies covering more than 2 million people and concluded that it may reduce (4) the risk of breast, gastric, colorectal, and colon cancer. The cancer mortality rate is significantly lower amongst those who eat this diet. This has been attributed to the higher intake of whole grains, vegetables, and fruits. The result of this study was published in the Nutrients journal.

   Another study according to the JAMA Internal Medicine journal discovered that women eating this diet were able to reduce the risk of breast cancer by 62%.

7. **Inflammation** – Fatty fish like tuna, mackerel, and salmon have a lot of omega-3 fatty acids that can reduce inflammation. Besides, the omega-3 will also improve the elasticity of your skin and make it stronger.

8. **Rheumatoid arthritis** – In this autoimmune disease, the body's immune system attacks the joints by mistake, causing swelling and pain. The National Institutes of Health's Office of Dietary Supplements has suggested that long-chain omega-3 fatty acids, which you will find in fatty fish provides relief from the symptoms of RA or Rheumatoid arthritis.

9. **Good for the gut** – The Med diet provides 7% more good bacteria in the microbiome, compared to those eating a traditional western diet as it is a plant-based eating plan with a lot of fruits, vegetables, nuts, seeds, and legumes. This improves gut health.

Several other scientific studies have also revealed the health gains of eating this diet.

The Rockefeller Foundation – This was one of the first studies on the diet carried out on the Greek island of Crete. The Greek government asked for help from the Rockefeller Foundation after the World War II because the island was severely destructed after the war and the people were in abject poverty. Many field staff were sent, including nutritionists and nurses.

They visited many homes and took notes on their food and drinking habits. To their surprise, it was found that most people were of good health and were living into old age in spite of the poverty. Very few people were suffering from heart disease, though 40% of their calories were coming from fat.

Ancel Keys' 7 Country Study – This was a follow-up study to find out the heart health condition of residents around the Mediterranean Sea. It was carried out in the late 1950s by Ancel Keys, the American scientist. In the late 1950s, 92 out of 1000 men in the United States were suffering from heart diseases. But in Crete, Ancel found to his surprise, that only 3 men out of 1000 had heart conditions.

The University of Barcelona Study – In recent time, the University of Barcelona
Carried out a study on 7000 men and women over 5 years. They found that there were significant improvements in heart health when the participants ate a Mediterranean diet. The risk of cardiovascular disease dropped by almost 30%. And they were also high-risk individuals, as the participants were all overweight people, and also diabetics and smokers. The results of this 2013 study was published by the New England Journal of Medicine.

The Cochrane Study – Carried out in the same year, this study too arrived at the same conclusion. The researchers concluded by noting that a high-protein, high-fiber, low-glycemic index, low-carbohydrate diet improves cardiovascular health and reduces the risk of diabetes.

Hundreds of studies have been carried out in recent years to verify whether the diet improves health or not. Almost all of them have concluded that those who eat a Mediterranean diet have lower risks of Alzheimer's, dementia, and diabetes. Many other health advantages have also been noted.

How to Get Started

The easiest way to start the diet is by making small changes. Gradually go deeper into the Mediterranean diet eating more of what is recommended and avoiding others.

Start by,

- Avoid butter. Sauté your food in olive oil instead.
- Include fresh vegetables and fruits in every meal. Eat fruits for dessert.
- Take fish instead of red meat. Choose fatty sea fish.
- Avoid refined bread, pasta, and rice. Eat whole-grains.
- Limit the intake of high-fat dairy products. Take only small amounts of cheese.
- Eat vegetarian or vegan once a week. Make this twice a week as you go deeper into the diet. Create your meals around vegetables, whole-grains, and beans. Add spices and herbs to make it more interesting.

Do Not Skip the Breakfast

Many people skip breakfast when they are rushing to work. This is never a good idea because your body will then think that food is scarce and slow down your metabolism, which may lead to weight gain.

You can eat English muffins, whole-grain toast, bagels with hummus, soft cheese, nut butter, or avocado. Add a cup of berries or a medium-sized fruit. The fiber will keep you full. You can also have some nuts and an egg. Bacon or sausage is allowed only a couple of times in a month. Things like a bowl of soup will also serve you well.

Dessert

The dessert you should eat in the Mediterranean diet is not the same as your typical American selection. For example, sweets and ice creams are not allowed. You should also restrict or avoid cakes, cookies, and pastries. At most, you can have them once or twice a month.

Eat fruits for dessert. You can be creative if you get bored with having fruits every day. For instance, you can grill pineapple and drizzle some honey on top. Stuff your date or fig with goat cheese. Sprinkle a few nuts. Poach your pear in pomegranate juice with some honey. You may also prepare a whole-wheat fruit tar. There are so many ways to make your dessert interesting.

In some Mediterranean cultures, they will have a glass of red wine after a meal. Research has suggested the health benefits of drinking red wine moderately, but not everyone is convinced. Do not start if you are not into wine drinking already.

Top 7 Success Tips to Live Mediterranean Diet Lifestyle

1. **Plan your meals** – Plan your meals in advance. Plan what you want to eat throughout the week when you have time during the weekend. This includes the snacks too. Then make sure that you have the necessary ingredients in advance. It will be easier for you to eat healthy throughout the week. You can even prepare a few meals in advance, especially those you can refrigerate.

2. **Cook with olive oil** – Don't use coconut oil or vegetable oil. Extra-virgin olive oil is strongly recommended. Olive oil provides monounsaturated fatty acids that will improve your HDL cholesterol level (the good type). A 2017 study even shows that HDL cholesterol can remove LDL particles from the arteries. Drizzle some olive oil on your food to improve flavor.

3. **Meat-free days** – The Med diet is mostly plant-based with some fish. Pulses, beans, and fish will give you all the proteins you need. Meat is only allowed once or twice a month. Chicken is better than red meat.

4. **Adopt** – Mediterranean flavors might not go precisely with all cuisines. However, you can still adopt many elements. For instance, while preparing something spicy like curry, you can use oils with unsaturated fats. Olive oil is the best. Sunflower and rapeseed oil is better than palm oil or coconut oil.

5. **Antioxidants** – Eat vegetables and fruits packed with antioxidants. This will give you pterostilbene, resveratrol, and glutathione. You will get glutathione from onions, garlic, cruciferous vegetables, and spinach. Raspberries and blueberries will provide resveratrol. Oregano, mint, basil and such other herbs will give you other key antioxidants for good health.

6. **Eat wholesome** – Pasta, an Italian favorite from the Mediterranean region, also fits into the plan. Prioritize whole-grain options, but you will find grain-free options as well to eliminate having more grains.

7. **Snacking** – Have nuts for snacks. Keep a handful of cashews, pistachios, or almonds with you. They are all very satisfying. The Nutrition Journal published a study where it was found that those who replaced chips, cookies, cereal bars, and crackers with almonds ended up adding fewer empty

calories, sodium, and added sugar. Nuts will also provide you with essential minerals and fiber.

Seven-Day Meal Plan

Day 1 –

Breakfast	Lunch	Dinner
Rainbow frittata 1 serving, or grilled tomatoes, whole-wheat toast, and 1 pan-fried eggs.	Green salad with hummus and pita bed – 1 serving, or 2 cups of salad greens with olives and cherry tomatoes on top.	Dijon Salmon with Green Bean Pilaf – 1 serving, or whole-grain pizza with green vegetables and tomato sauce. Add tuna, ham, or chicken for more calories.

Day 2 –

Breakfast	Lunch	Dinner
Muesli with raspberries 1 serving, or 1 cup Greek yogurt. You can also have ½ cup blueberries or chopped nectarines.	Brussels sprout salad with chickpeas – 1 serving, or a whole-grain sandwich with vegetables like zucchini, eggplant, onion, and bell pepper. Spread avocado or hummus on your bread for more calories.	Linguine with mushroom sauce – 1 serving, or salmon/baked cod 1 portion with black pepper and garlic for flavor. You can also eat 1 roasted potato with chives.

Day 3 –

Breakfast	Lunch	Dinner
Ricotta and fig toast 1 serving, or 1 cup whole-grain oats with dates, honey, and cinnamon. Have 1 oz. shredded almonds too.	Boiled beans with spices like garlic, cumin, and laurel. Also have a cup of arugula with toppings of cucumber, feta cheese, tomato, and olive oil dressing.	1 serving of quinoa or cod in tomato sauce. Alternatively, you can have half cup whole-grain pasta with olive oil, grilled vegetables, and tomato sauce.

Day 4 –

Breakfast	Lunch	Dinner
Creamy pecan, blueberry oats 1 serving, or 2 scrambled eggs with onions, tomatoes, and bell peppers.	You can have a serving of Brussels sprouts salad or roasted anchovies on whole-grain toast with some lemon juice. Have 2 cups of steamed tomatoes and kale.	1 serving of quinoa chickpea bowl, or 1 cups of spinach with herbs and lemon juice. Add boiled artichoke with salt, garlic powder, and olive oil.

Day 5 –

Breakfast	Lunch	Dinner
Muesli with raspberries 1 serving, or 1 cup Greek yogurt with honey and cinnamon. Add a chopped apple if you want.	Chicken pasta with garlic, tomatoes, red pepper, basil, baby spinach, and Italian seasoning, or a cup of quinoa with tomatoes, olives, and bell peppers.	Stuffed olive cod with oregano and lemon or 2 cups steamed kale with cucumber, tomato, lemon juice, Parmesan cheese, and olives.

Day 6 –

Breakfast	Lunch	Dinner
Med cheese and broccoli omelet with Romano cheese, broccoli florets, 2% milk, parsley, and eggs, or 2 slices of whole-grain toast with a soft cheese like queso fresco or ricotta.	Cobb salad with parsley, cucumber, yogurt, baby spinach, eggs, avocado, tomatoes, bacon strips, and feta cheese, or 1 cups mixed greens with cucumber and tomato.	Shrimp skillet with oregano, garlic, onion, olive oil, tomatoes, parsley, shrimp, and feta cheese, or oven-roasted veggies like carrot, artichoke, eggplant, zucchini, tomato, and sweet potatoes.

Day 7 –

Breakfast	Lunch	Dinner
Tomato bites with basil, oregano, Gouda cheese, and olives, or yogurt and honey fruit cups with orange zest, almond, and fruits like	Mediterranean chickpeas with garlic, onion, olive oil, artichoke, oregano, lemon juice, and tomatoes, or stewed zucchini, onion, potato, and	1 serving of Mediterranean chicken and orzo, or 2 cups greens like spinach or arugula with olives, olive oil, and tomato. You can also

bananas, grapes, apples, and pears.	squash in a herb and tomato sauce.	add a small white fish portion.

Chapter 2 - Egg Recipes

Breakfast Egg on Avocado

Serves: 6 , Cooking Time: 15 minutes

Ingredients:

- 1 tsp garlic powder
- 1/2 tsp sea salt
- 1/4 cup Parmesan cheese (grated or shredded)
- 1/4 tsp black pepper
- 3 medium avocados (cut in half, pitted, skin on)
- 6 medium eggs

Directions for Cooking:

1) Prepare muffin tins and preheat the oven to 350°F.
2) To ensure that the egg would fit inside the cavity of the avocado, lightly scrape off 1/3 of the meat.
3) Place avocado on muffin tin to ensure that it faces with the top up.
4) Evenly season each avocado with pepper, salt, and garlic powder.
5) Add one egg on each avocado cavity and garnish tops with cheese.
6) Pop in the oven and bake until the egg white is set, about 15 minutes.
7) Serve and enjoy.

Nutrition Information:

Calories per serving: 252; Protein: 14.0g; Carbs: 4.0g; Fat: 20.0g

Breakfast Egg-artichoke Casserole

Serves: 8 , Cooking Time: 35 minutes

Ingredients:

- 16 large eggs
- 14 ounce can artichoke hearts, drained
- 10-ounce box frozen chopped spinach, thawed and drained well
- 1 cup shredded white cheddar
- 1 garlic clove, minced
- 1 teaspoon salt
- 1/2 cup parmesan cheese
- 1/2 cup ricotta cheese
- 1/2 teaspoon dried thyme
- 1/2 teaspoon crushed red pepper
- 1/4 cup milk
- 1/4 cup shaved onion

Directions for Cooking:

1) Lightly grease a 9x13-inch baking dish with cooking spray and preheat the oven to 350oF.
2) In a large mixing bowl, add eggs and milk. Mix thoroughly.
3) With a paper towel, squeeze out the excess moisture from the spinach leaves and add to the bowl of eggs.
4) Into small pieces, break the artichoke hearts and separate the leaves. Add to the bowl of eggs.
5) Except for the ricotta cheese, add remaining ingredients in the bowl of eggs and mix thoroughly.
6) Pour egg mixture into the prepared dish.
7) Evenly add dollops of ricotta cheese on top of the eggs and then pop in the oven.
8) Bake until eggs are set and doesn't jiggle when shook, about 35 minutes.
9) Remove from the oven and evenly divide into suggested servings. Enjoy.

Nutrition Information:

Calories per serving: 302; Protein: 22.6g; Carbs: 10.8g; Fat: 18.7g

Brekky Egg-potato Hash

Serves: 2, Cooking Time: 25 minutes

Ingredients:

- 1 zucchini, diced
- 1/2 cup chicken broth
- ½ pound cooked chicken
- 1 tablespoon olive oil
- 4 ounces shrimp
- Salt and ground black pepper to taste
- 1 large sweet potato, diced
- 2 eggs
- 1/4 teaspoon cayenne pepper
- 2 teaspoons garlic powder
- 1 cup fresh spinach (optional)

Directions for Cooking:

1) In a skillet, add the olive oil.
2) Fry the shrimp, cooked chicken and sweet potato for 2 minutes.
3) Add the cayenne pepper, garlic powder and salt, and toss for 4 minutes.
4) Add the zucchini and toss for another 3 minutes.
5) Whisk the eggs in a bowl and add to the skillet.
6) Season using salt and pepper. Cover with the lid.
7) Cook for 1 minute and add the chicken broth.
8) Cover and cook for another 8 minutes on high heat.
9) Add the spinach and toss for 2 more minutes.
10) Serve immediately.

Nutrition Information:

Calories per serving: 190; Protein: 11.7g; Carbs: 2.9g; Fat: 12.3g

Dill and Tomato Frittata

Serves: 6, Cooking Time: 35 minutes

Ingredients:

- Pepper and salt to taste
- 1 tsp red pepper flakes
- 2 garlic cloves, minced
- ½ cup crumbled goat cheese – optional
- 2 tbsp fresh chives, chopped
- 2 tbsp fresh dill, chopped
- 4 tomatoes, diced
- 8 eggs, whisked
- 1 tsp coconut oil

Directions for Cooking:

1) Grease a 9-inch round baking pan and preheat oven to 325oF.
2) In a large bowl, mix well all ingredients and pour into prepped pan.
3) Pop into the oven and bake until middle is cooked through around 30-35 minutes.
4) Remove from oven and garnish with more chives and dill.

Nutrition Information:

Calories per serving: 149; Protein: 13.26g; Carbs: 9.93g; Fat: 10.28g

Paleo Almond Banana Pancakes

Serves: 3, Cooking Time: 10 minutes

Ingredients:

- ¼ cup almond flour
- ½ teaspoon ground cinnamon
- 3 eggs
- 1 banana, mashed
- 1 tablespoon almond butter
- 1 teaspoon vanilla extract
- 1 teaspoon olive oil
- Sliced banana to serve

Directions for Cooking:

1) Whisk the eggs in a mixing bowl until they become fluffy.
2) In another bowl, mash the banana using a fork and add to the egg mixture.
3) Add the vanilla, almond butter, cinnamon and almond flour.
4) Mix into a smooth batter.
5) Heat the olive oil in a skillet.
6) Add one spoonful of the batter and fry them on both sides.
7) Keep doing these steps until you are done with all the batter.
8) Add some sliced banana on top before serving.

Nutrition Information:

Calories per serving: 306; Protein: 14.4g; Carbs: 3.6g; Fat: 26.0g

Chapter 3 Vegetable Recipes

Banana-Coconut Breakfast

Serves: 4, Cooking Time: 3 minutes

Ingredients:

- 1 ripe banana
- 1 cup desiccated coconut
- 1 cup coconut milk
- 3 tablespoons raisins, chopped
- 2 tablespoon ground flax seed
- 1 teaspoon vanilla
- A dash of cinnamon
- A dash of nutmeg
- Salt to taste

Directions for Cooking:

1) Place all ingredients in a deep pan.
2) Allow to simmer for 3 minutes on low heat.
3) Place in individual containers.
4) Put a label and store in the fridge.
5) Allow to thaw at room temperature before heating in the microwave oven.

Nutrition Information:

Calories per serving:279; Carbs: 25.46g; Protein: 6.4g; Fat: g; Fiber: 5.9g

Basil and Tomato Soup

Serves: 2, Cooking Time: 25 minutes

Ingredients:

- Salt and pepper to taste
- 2 bay leaves
- 1 ½ cups almond milk, unsweetened
- ½ tsp raw apple cider vinegar
- 1/3 cup basil leaves
- ¼ cup tomato paste
- 3 cups tomatoes, chopped
- 1 medium celery stalk, chopped
- 1 medium carrot, chopped
- 1 medium garlic clove, minced
- ½ cup white onion
- 2 tbsp vegetable broth

Directions for Cooking:

1) Heat the vegetable broth in a large saucepan over medium heat.
2) Add the onions and cook for 3 minutes. Add the garlic and cook for another minute.
3) Add the celery and carrots and cook for 1 minute.
4) Mix in the tomatoes and bring to a boil. Simmer for 15 minutes.
5) Add the almond milk, basil and bay leaves. Season with salt and pepper to taste.

Nutrition Information:

Calories per Serving: 213; Carbs: 42.0g; Protein: 6.9g; Fat: 3.9g

Butternut Squash Hummus

Serves: 8, Cooking Time: 15 minutes

Ingredients:

- 2 pounds butternut squash, seeded and peeled
- 1 tablespoon olive oil
- ¼ cup tahini
- 2 tablespoons lemon juice
- 2 cloves of garlic, minced
- Salt and pepper to taste

Directions for Cooking:

1) Heat the oven to 3000F.
2) Coat the butternut squash with olive oil.
3) Place in a baking dish and bake for 15 minutes in the oven.
4) Once the squash is cooked, place in a food processor together with the rest of the ingredients.
5) Pulse until smooth.
6) Place in individual containers.
7) Put a label and store in the fridge.
8) Allow to warm at room temperature before heating in the microwave oven.
9) Serve with carrots or celery sticks.

Nutrition Information:

Calories per serving: 115; Carbs: 15.8g; Protein: 2.5g; Fat:5.8g; Fiber: 6.7g

Cajun Jambalaya Soup

Serves: 6, Cooking Time: 6 hours

Ingredients:

- ¼ cup Frank's red hot sauce
- 3 tbsp Cajun seasoning
- 2 cups okra
- ½ head of cauliflower
- 1 pkg spicy Andouille sausages
- 4 oz chicken, diced
- 1 lb. large shrimps, raw and deveined
- 2 bay leaves
- 2 cloves garlic, diced
- 1 large can organic diced tomatoes
- 1 large onion, chopped
- 4 pepper
- 5 cups chicken stock

Directions for Cooking:

1) In slow cooker, place the bay leaves, red hot sauce, Cajun seasoning, chicken, garlic, onions, and peppers.
2) Set slow cooker on low and cook for 5 ½ hours.
3) Then add sausages cook for 10 minutes.
4) Meanwhile, pulse cauliflower in food processor to make cauliflower rice.
5) Add cauliflower rice into slow cooker. Cook for 20 minutes.
6) Serve and enjoy.

Nutrition Information:

Calories per Serving: 155; Carbs: 13.9g; Protein: 17.4g; Fat: 3.8g

Collard Green Wrap Greek Style

Serves: 4, Cooking Time: 0 minutes

Wrap Ingredients:

- ½ block feta, cut into 4 (1-inch thick) strips (4-oz)
- ½ cup purple onion, diced
- ½ medium red bell pepper, julienned
- 1 medium cucumber, julienned
- 4 large cherry tomatoes, halved
- 4 large collard green leaves, washed
- 8 whole kalamata olives, halved

Tzatziki Sauce Ingredients:

- 1 cup full-fat plain Greek yogurt
- 1 tablespoon white vinegar
- 1 teaspoon garlic powder
- 2 tablespoons minced fresh dill
- 2 tablespoons olive oil
- 2.5-ounces cucumber, seeded and grated (¼-whole)
- Salt and pepper to taste

Directions for Cooking:

1) Make the Tzatziki sauce first: make sure to squeeze out all the excess liquid from the cucumber after grating. In a small bowl, mix all sauce ingredients thoroughly and refrigerate.
2) Prepare and slice all wrap ingredients.
3) On a flat surface, spread one collard green leaf. Spread 2 tablespoons of Tzatziki sauce on middle of the leaf.
4) Layer ¼ of each of the tomatoes, feta, olives, onion, pepper, and cucumber. Place them on the center of the leaf, like piling them high instead of spreading them.
5) Fold the leaf like you would a burrito. Repeat process for remaining ingredients.
6) Serve and enjoy.

Nutrition Information:

Calories per serving: 165.3; Protein: 7.0g; Carbs: 9.9g; Fat: 11.2g

Portobello Mushroom Pizza

Serves: 4, Cooking Time: 12 minutes

Ingredients:

- ½ teaspoon red pepper flakes
- A handful of fresh basil, chopped
- 1 can black olives, chopped
- 1 medium onion, chopped
- 1 green pepper, chopped
- ¼ cup chopped roasted yellow peppers
- ½ cup prepared nut cheese, shredded
- 2 cups prepared gluten-free pizza sauce
- 8 Portobello mushrooms, cleaned and stems removed

Directions for Cooking:

1) Preheat the oven toaster.
2) Take a baking sheet and grease it. Set aside.
3) Place the Portobello mushroom cap-side down and spoon 2 tablespoon of packaged pizza sauce on the underside of each cap. Add nut cheese and top with the remaining ingredients.
4) Broil for 12 minutes or until the toppings are wilted.

Nutrition Information:

Calories per Serving: 578; Carbs: 73.0g; Protein: 24.4g; Fat: 22.4g

Roasted Root Veggies

Serves: 6, Cooking Time: 1 hour and 30 minutes

Ingredients:

- 2 tbsp olive oil
- 1 head garlic, cloves separated and peeled
- 1 large turnip, peeled and cut into ½-inch pieces
- 1 medium sized red onion, cut into ½-inch pieces
- 1 ½ lbs. beets, trimmed but not peeled, scrubbed and cut into ½-inch pieces
- 1 ½ lbs. Yukon gold potatoes, unpeeled, cut into ½-inch pieces
- 2 ½ lbs. butternut squash, peeled, seeded, cut into ½-inch pieces

Directions for Cooking:

1) Grease 2 rimmed and large baking sheets. Preheat oven to 425oF.
2) In a large bowl, mix all ingredients thoroughly.
3) Into the two baking sheets, evenly divide the root vegetables, spread in one layer.
4) Season generously with pepper and salt.
5) Pop into the oven and roast for 1 hour and 15 minute or until golden brown and tender.
6) Remove from oven and let it cool for at least 15 minutes before serving.

Nutrition Information:

Calories per Serving: 298; Carbs: 61.1g; Protein: 7.4g; Fat: 5.0g

Amazingly Good Parsley Tabbouleh

Serves: 4, Cooking Time: 15 minutes

Ingredients:

- ¼ cup chopped fresh mint
- ¼ cup lemon juice
- ¼ tsp salt
- ½ cup bulgur
- ½ tsp minced garlic
- 1 cup water
- 1 small cucumber, peeled, seeded and diced
- 2 cups finely chopped flat-leaf parsley
- 2 tbsp extra virgin olive oil
- 2 tomatoes, diced
- 4 scallions, thinly sliced
- Pepper to taste

Directions for Cooking:

1) Cook bulgur according to package instructions. Drain and set aside to cool for at least 15 minutes.
2) In a small bowl, mix pepper, salt, garlic, oil, and lemon juice.
3) Transfer bulgur into a large salad bowl and mix in scallions, cucumber, tomatoes, mint, and parsley.
4) Pour in dressing and toss well to coat.
5) Place bowl in ref until chilled before serving.

Nutrition Information:

Calories per Serving: 134.8; Carbs: 13g; Protein: 7.2g; Fat: 6g

Appetizing Mushroom Lasagna

Serves: 8, Cooking Time: 75 minutes

Ingredients:

- ½ cup grated Parmigiano-Reggiano cheese
- No boil lasagna noodles
- Cooking spray
- ¼ cup all-purpose flour
- 3 cups reduced fat milk, divided
- 2 tbsp chopped fresh chives, divided
- 1/3 cup less fat cream cheese
- ½ cup white wine
- 6 garlic cloves, minced and divided
- 1 ½ tbsp. Chopped fresh thyme
- ½ tsp freshly ground black pepper, divided
- 1 tsp salt, divided
- 1 package 4 oz pre-sliced exotic mushroom blend
- 1 package 8oz pre-sliced cremini mushrooms
- 1 ¼ cups chopped shallots
- 2 tbsp olive oil, divided
- 1 tbsp butter
- 1 oz dried porcini mushrooms
- 1 cup boiling water

Directions for Cooking:

1) For 30 minutes, submerge porcini in 1 cup boiling hot water. With a sieve, strain mushroom and reserve liquid.

2) Over medium high fire, melt butter on a fry pan. Mix in 2 tbsp oil and for three minutes fry shallots. Add ¼ tsp pepper, ½ tsp salt, exotic mushrooms and cremini, cook for six minutes. Stir in 3 garlic cloves and thyme, cook for a minute. Bring to a boil as you pour wine by increasing fire to high and cook until liquid evaporates around a minute. Turn off fire and stir in porcini mushrooms, 1 tbsp chives and cream cheese. Mix well.

3) On medium high fire, place a separate medium sized pan with 1 tbsp oil. Sauté for half a minute 3 garlic cloves. Then bring to a boil as you pour 2 ¾ cups milk and reserved porcini liquid. Season with remaining pepper and salt. In a separate bowl,

whisk together flour and ¼ cup milk and pour into pan. Stir constantly and cook until mixture thickens.

4) In a greased rectangular glass dish, pour and spread ½ cup of sauce, top with lasagna, top with half of mushroom mixture and another layer of lasagna. Repeat the layering process and instead of lasagna layer, end with the mushroom mixture and cover with cheese.

5) For 45 minutes, bake the lasagna in a preheated 350oF oven. Garnish with chives before serving.

Nutrition Information:

Calories per Serving: 268; Carbs: 29.6g; Protein: 10.2g; Fat: 12.6g

Artichokes, Olives & Tuna Pasta

Serves: 4, Cooking Time: 15 minutes

Ingredients:

- ¼ cup chopped fresh basil
- ¼ cup chopped green olives
- ¼ tsp freshly ground pepper
- ½ cup white wine
- ½ tsp salt, divided
- 1 10-oz package frozen artichoke hearts, thawed and squeezed dry
- 2 cups grape tomatoes, halved
- 2 tbsp lemon juice
- 2 tsp chopped fresh rosemary
- 2 tsp freshly grated lemon zest
- 3 cloves garlic, minced
- 4 tbsp extra virgin olive oil, divided
- 6-oz whole wheat penne pasta
- 8-oz tuna steak, cut into 3 pieces

Directions for Cooking:

1) Cook penne pasta according to package instructions. Drain and set aside.
2) Preheat grill to medium high.
3) In bowl, toss and mix ¼ tsp pepper, ¼ tsp salt, 1 tsp rosemary, lemon zest, 1 tbsp oil and tuna pieces.
4) Grill tuna for 3 minutes per side. Allow to cool and flake into bite sized pieces.
5) On medium fire, place a large nonstick saucepan and heat 3 tbsp oil.
6) Sauté remaining rosemary, garlic olives, and artichoke hearts for 4 minutes
7) Add wine and tomatoes, bring to a boil and cook for 3 minutes while stirring once in a while.
8) Add remaining salt, lemon juice, tuna pieces and pasta. Cook until heated through.
9) To serve, garnish with basil and enjoy.

Nutrition Information:

Calories per Serving: 127.6; Carbs: 13g; Protein: 7.2g; Fat: 5.2g

Chapter 4 Pasta, Rice and Grains Recipes

Bell Peppers 'n Tomato-Chickpea Rice

Serves: 4, Cooking Time: 35 minutes

Ingredients:

- 2 tablespoons olive oil
- 1/2 chopped red bell pepper
- 1/2 chopped green bell pepper
- 1/2 chopped yellow pepper
- 1/2 chopped red pepper
- 1 medium onion, chopped
- 1 clove garlic, minced
- 2 cups cooked jasmine rice
- 1 teaspoon tomato paste
- 1 cup chickpeas
- salt to taste
- 1/2 teaspoon paprika
- 1 small tomato, chopped
- Parsley for garnish

Directions for Cooking:

1) In a large mixing bowl, whisk well olive oil, garlic, tomato paste, and paprika. Season with salt generously.
2) Mix in rice and toss well to coat in the dressing.
3) Add remaining ingredients and toss well to mix.
4) Let salad rest to allow flavors to mix for 15 minutes.
5) Toss one more time and adjust salt to taste if needed.
6) Garnish with parsley and serve.

Nutrition Information:

Calories per serving: 490; Carbs: 93.0g; Protein: 10.0g; Fat: 8.0g

Seafood and Veggie Pasta

Serves: 4, Cooking Time: 20 minutes

Ingredients:

- ¼ tsp pepper
- ¼ tsp salt
- 1 lb raw shelled shrimp
- 1 lemon, cut into wedges
- 1 tbsp butter
- 1 tbsp olive oil
- 2 5-oz cans chopped clams, drained (reserve 2 tbsp clam juice)
- 2 tbsp dry white wine
- 4 cloves garlic, minced
- 4 cups zucchini, spiraled (use a veggie spiralizer)
- 4 tbsp Parmesan Cheese
- Chopped fresh parsley to garnish

Directions for Cooking:

1) Ready the zucchini and spiralize with a veggie spiralizer. Arrange 1 cup of zucchini noodle per bowl. Total of 4 bowls.
2) On medium fire, place a large nonstick saucepan and heat oil and butter.
3) For a minute, sauté garlic. Add shrimp and cook for 3 minutes until opaque or cooked.
4) Add white wine, reserved clam juice and clams. Bring to a simmer and continue simmering for 2 minutes or until half of liquid has evaporated. Stir constantly.
5) Season with pepper and salt. And if needed add more to taste.
6) Remove from fire and evenly distribute seafood sauce to 4 bowls.
7) Top with a tablespoonful of Parmesan cheese per bowl, serve and enjoy.

Nutrition Information:

Calories per Serving: 324.9; Carbs: 12g; Protein: 43.8g; Fat: 11.3g

Breakfast Salad From Grains and Fruits

Serves: 6 , Cooking Time: 20 minutes

Ingredients:

- ¼ tsp salt
- ¾ cup bulgur
- ¾ cup quick cooking brown rice
- 1 8-oz low fat vanilla yogurt
- 1 cup raisins
- 1 Granny Smith apple
- 1 orange
- 1 Red delicious apple
- 3 cups water

Directions for Cooking:

1) On high fire, place a large pot and bring water to a boil.
2) Add bulgur and rice. Lower fire to a simmer and cook for ten minutes while covered.
3) Turn off fire, set aside for 2 minutes while covered.
4) In baking sheet, transfer and evenly spread grains to cool.
5) Meanwhile, peel oranges and cut into sections. Chop and core apples.
6) Once grains are cool, transfer to a large serving bowl along with fruits.
7) Add yogurt and mix well to coat.
8) Serve and enjoy.

Nutrition Information:

Calories per Serving: 48.6; Carbs: 23.9g; Protein: 3.7g; Fat: 1.1g

Puttanesca Style Bucatini

Serves: 4, Cooking Time: 40 minutes

Ingredients:

- 1 tbsp capers, rinsed
- 1 tsp coarsely chopped fresh oregano
- 1 tsp finely chopped garlic
- 1/8 tsp salt
- 12-oz bucatini pasta
- 2 cups coarsely chopped canned no-salt-added whole peeled tomatoes with their juice
- 3 tbsp extra virgin olive oil, divided
- 4 anchovy fillets, chopped
- 8 black Kalamata olives, pitted and sliced into slivers

Directions for Cooking:

1) Cook bucatini pasta according to package directions. Drain, keep warm, and set aside.
2) On medium fire, place a large nonstick saucepan and heat 2 tbsp oil.
3) Sauté anchovies until it starts to disintegrate.
4) Add garlic and sauté for 15 seconds.
5) Add tomatoes, sauté for 15 to 20 minutes or until no longer watery. Season with 1/8 tsp salt.
6) Add oregano, capers, and olives.
7) Add pasta, sautéing until heated through.
8) To serve, drizzle pasta with remaining olive oil and enjoy.

Nutrition Information:

Calories per Serving: 207.4; Carbs: 31g; Protein: 5.1g; Fat: 7g

Cinnamon Quinoa Bars

Serves: 4, Cooking Time: 30 minutes

Ingredients:

- 2 ½ cups cooked quinoa
- 4 large eggs
- 1/3 cup unsweetened almond milk
- 1/3 cup pure maple syrup
- Seeds from ½ whole vanilla bean pod or 1 tbsp vanilla extract
- 1 ½ tbsp cinnamon
- 1/4 tsp salt

Directions for Cooking:

1) Preheat oven to 375oF.
2) Combine all ingredients into large bowl and mix well.
3) In an 8 x 8 Baking pan, cover with parchment paper.
4) Pour batter evenly into baking dish.
5) Bake for 25-30 minutes or until it has set. It should not wiggle when you lightly shake the pan because the eggs are fully cooked.
6) Remove as quickly as possible from pan and parchment paper onto cooling rack.
7) Cut into 4 pieces.
8) Enjoy on its own, with a small spread of almond or nut butter or wait until it cools to enjoy the next morning.

Nutrition Information:

Calories per serving: 285; Carbs: 46.2g; Protein: 8.5g; Fat: 7.4g

Creamy Alfredo Fettuccine

Serves: 4, Cooking Time: 25 minutes

Ingredients:

- Grated parmesan cheese
- ½ cup freshly grated parmesan cheese
- 1/8 tsp freshly ground black pepper
- ½ tsp salt
- 1 cup whipping cream
- 2 tbsp butter
- 8 oz dried fettuccine, cooked and drained

Directions for Cooking:

1) On medium high fire, place a big fry pan and heat butter.
2) Add pepper, salt and cream and gently boil for three to five minutes.
3) Once thickened, turn off fire and quickly stir in ½ cup of parmesan cheese. Toss in pasta, mix well.
4) Top with another batch of parmesan cheese and serve.

Nutrition Information:

Calories per Serving: 202; Carbs: 21.1g; Protein: 7.9g; Fat: 10.2g

Greek Couscous Salad and Herbed Lamb Chops

Serves: 4, Cooking Time: 30 minutes

Ingredients:

- ¼ tsp salt
- ½ cup crumbled feta
- ½ cup whole wheat couscous
- 1 cup water
- 1 medium cucumber, peeled and chopped
- 1 tbsp finely chopped fresh parsley
- 1 tbsp minced garlic
- 2 ½ lbs. lamb loin chops, trimmed of fat
- 2 medium tomatoes, chopped
- 2 tbsp finely chopped fresh dill
- 2 tsp extra virgin olive oil
- 3 tbsp lemon juice

Directions for Cooking:

1) On medium saucepan, add water and bring to a boil.
2) In a small bowl, mix salt, parsley, and garlic. Rub onto lamb chops.
3) On medium high fire, place a large nonstick saucepan and heat oil.
4) Pan fry lamb chops for 5 minutes per side or to desired doneness. Once done, turn off fire and keep warm.
5) On saucepan of boiling water, add couscous. Once boiling, lower fire to a simmer, cover and cook for two minutes.
6) After two minutes, turn off fire, cover and let it stand for 5 minutes.
7) Fluff couscous with a fork and place into a medium bowl.
8) Add dill, lemon juice, feta, cucumber, and tomatoes in bowl of couscous and toss well to combine.
9) Serve lamb chops with a side of couscous and enjoy.

Nutrition Information:

Calories per Serving: 524.1; Carbs: 12.3g; Protein: 61.8g; Fat: 25.3g

Spanish Rice Casserole with Cheesy Beef

Serves: 2, Cooking Time: 32 minutes

Ingredients:

- 2 tablespoons chopped green bell pepper
- 1/4 teaspoon Worcestershire sauce
- 1/4 teaspoon ground cumin
- 1/4 cup shredded Cheddar cheese
- 1/4 cup finely chopped onion
- 1/4 cup chile sauce
- 1/3 cup uncooked long grain rice
- 1/2-pound lean ground beef
- 1/2 teaspoon salt
- 1/2 teaspoon brown sugar
- 1/2 pinch ground black pepper
- 1/2 cup water
- 1/2 (14.5 ounce) can canned tomatoes
- 1 tablespoon chopped fresh cilantro

Directions for Cooking:

1) Place a nonstick saucepan on medium fire and brown beef for 10 minutes while crumbling beef. Discard fat.
2) Stir in pepper, Worcestershire sauce, cumin, brown sugar, salt, chile sauce, rice, water, tomatoes, green bell pepper, and onion. Mix well and cook for 10 minutes until blended and a bit tender.
3) Transfer to an ovenproof casserole and press down firmly. Sprinkle cheese on top and cook for 7 minutes at 400oF preheated oven. Broil for 3 minutes until top is lightly browned.
4) Serve and enjoy with chopped cilantro.

Nutrition Information:

Calories per serving: 460; Carbohydrates: 35.8g; Protein: 37.8g; Fat: 17.9g

Tasty Lasagna Rolls

Serves: 6, Cooking Time: 20 minutes

Ingredients:

- ¼ tsp crushed red pepper
- ¼ tsp salt
- ½ cup shredded mozzarella cheese
- ½ cups parmesan cheese, shredded
- 1 14-oz package tofu, cubed
- 1 25-oz can of low-sodium marinara sauce
- 1 tbsp extra virgin olive oil
- 12 whole wheat lasagna noodles
- 2 tbsp Kalamata olives, chopped
- 3 cloves minced garlic
- 3 cups spinach, chopped

Directions for Cooking:

1) Put enough water on a large pot and cook the lasagna noodles according to package instructions. Drain, rinse and set aside until ready to use.
2) In a large skillet, sauté garlic over medium heat for 20 seconds. Add the tofu and spinach and cook until the spinach wilts. Transfer this mixture in a bowl and add parmesan olives, salt, red pepper and 2/3 cup of the marinara sauce.
3) In a pan, spread a cup of marinara sauce on the bottom. To make the rolls, place noodle on a surface and spread ¼ cup of the tofu filling. Roll up and place it on the pan with the marinara sauce. Do this procedure until all lasagna noodles are rolled.
4) Place the pan over high heat and bring to a simmer. Reduce the heat to medium and let it cook for three more minutes. Sprinkle mozzarella cheese and let the cheese melt for two minutes. Serve hot.

Nutrition Information:

Calories per Serving: 304; Carbs: 39.2g; Protein: 23g; Fat: 19.2g

Tortellini Salad with Broccoli

Serves: 12, Cooking Time: 20 minutes

Ingredients:

- 1 red onion, chopped finely
- 1 cup sunflower seeds
- 1 cup raisins
- 3 heads fresh broccoli, cut into florets
- 2 tsp cider vinegar
- ½ cup white sugar
- ½ cup mayonnaise
- 20-oz fresh cheese filled tortellini

Directions for Cooking:

1) In a large pot of boiling water, cook tortellini according to manufacturer's instructions. Drain and rinse with cold water and set aside.
2) Whisk vinegar, sugar and mayonnaise to create your salad dressing.
3) Mix together in a large bowl red onion, sunflower seeds, raisins, tortellini and broccoli. Pour dressing and toss to coat.
4) Serve and enjoy.

Nutrition Information:

Calories per Serving: 272; Carbs: 38.7g; Protein: 5.0g; Fat: 8.1g

Simple Penne Anti-Pasto

Serves: 4, Cooking Time: 15 minutes

Ingredients:

- ¼ cup pine nuts, toasted
- ½ cup grated Parmigiano-Reggiano cheese, divided
- 8oz penne pasta, cooked and drained
- 1 6oz jar drained, sliced, marinated and quartered artichoke hearts
- 1 7 oz jar drained and chopped sun-dried tomato halves packed in oil
- 3 oz chopped prosciutto
- 1/3 cup pesto
- ½ cup pitted and chopped Kalamata olives
- 1 medium red bell pepper

Directions for Cooking:

1) Slice bell pepper, discard membranes, seeds and stem. On a foiled lined baking sheet, place bell pepper halves, press down by hand and broil in oven for eight minutes. Remove from oven, put in a sealed bag for 5 minutes before peeling and chopping.
2) Place chopped bell pepper in a bowl and mix in artichokes, tomatoes, prosciutto, pesto and olives.
3) Toss in ¼ cup cheese and pasta. Transfer to a serving dish and garnish with ¼ cup cheese and pine nuts. Serve and enjoy!

Nutrition Information:

Calories per Serving: 606; Carbs: 70.3g; Protein: 27.2g; Fat: 27.6g

Red Quinoa Peach Porridge

Serves: 1, Cooking Time: 30 minutes

Ingredients:

- ¼ cup old fashioned rolled oats
- ¼ cup red quinoa
- ½ cup milk
- 1 ½ cups water
- 2 peaches, peeled and sliced

Directions for Cooking:

1) On a small saucepan, place the peaches and quinoa. Add water and cook for 30 minutes.
2) Add the oatmeal and milk last and cook until the oats become tender.
3) Stir occasionally to avoid the porridge from sticking on the bottom of the pan.

Nutrition Information:

Calories per Serving: 456.6; Carbs: 77.3g; Protein: 16.6g; Fat: 9g

Chapter 5 Breads, Flatbreads, Pizzas Recipes

Avocado and Turkey Mix Panini

Serves: 2, Cooking Time: 8 minutes

Ingredients:

- 2 red peppers, roasted and sliced into strips
- ¼ lb. thinly sliced mesquite smoked turkey breast
- 1 cup whole fresh spinach leaves, divided
- 2 slices provolone cheese
- 1 tbsp olive oil, divided
- 2 ciabatta rolls
- ¼ cup mayonnaise
- ½ ripe avocado

Directions for Cooking:

1) In a bowl, mash thoroughly together mayonnaise and avocado. Then preheat Panini press.
2) Slice the bread rolls in half and spread olive oil on the insides of the bread. Then fill it with filling, layering them as you go: provolone, turkey breast, roasted red pepper, spinach leaves and spread avocado mixture and cover with the other bread slice.
3) Place sandwich in the Panini press and grill for 5 to 8 minutes until cheese has melted and bread is crisped and ridged.

Nutrition Information:

Calories per Serving: 546; Carbs: 31.9g; Protein: 27.8g; Fat: 34.8g

Cucumber, Chicken and Mango Wrap

Serves: 1, Cooking Time: 20 minutes

Ingredients:

- ½ of a medium cucumber cut lengthwise
- ½ of ripe mango
- 1 tbsp salad dressing of choice
- 1 whole wheat tortilla wrap
- 1-inch thick slice of chicken breast around 6-inch in length
- 2 tbsp oil for frying
- 2 tbsp whole wheat flour
- 2 to 4 lettuce leaves
- Salt and pepper to taste

Directions for Cooking:

1) Slice a chicken breast into 1-inch strips and just cook a total of 6-inch strips. That would be like two strips of chicken. Store remaining chicken for future use.
2) Season chicken with pepper and salt. Dredge in whole wheat flour.
3) On medium fire, place a small and nonstick fry pan and heat oil. Once oil is hot, add chicken strips and fry until golden brown around 5 minutes per side.
4) While chicken is cooking, place tortilla wraps in oven and cook for 3 to 5 minutes. Then remove from oven and place on a plate.
5) Slice cucumber lengthwise, use only ½ of it and store remaining cucumber. Peel cucumber cut into quarter and remove pith. Place the two slices of cucumber on the tortilla wrap, 1-inch away from the edge.
6) Slice mango and store the other half with seed. Peel the mango without seed, slice into strips and place on top of the cucumber on the tortilla wrap.
7) Once chicken is cooked, place chicken beside the cucumber in a line.
8) Add cucumber leaf, drizzle with salad dressing of choice.
9) Roll the tortilla wrap, serve and enjoy.

Nutrition Information:

Calories per Serving: 434; Fat: 10g; Protein: 21g; Carbohydrates: 65g

Fattoush Salad –middle East Bread Salad

Serves: 6, Cooking Time: 15 minutes

Ingredients:

- 2 loaves pita bread
- 1 tbsp Extra Virgin Olive Oil
- 1/2 tsp sumac, more for later
- Salt and pepper
- 1 heart of Romaine lettuce, chopped
- 1 English cucumber, chopped
- 5 Roma tomatoes, chopped
- 5 green onions (both white and green parts), chopped
- 5 radishes, stems removed, thinly sliced
- 2 cups chopped fresh parsley leaves, stems removed
- 1 cup chopped fresh mint leaves

Dressing Ingredients:

- 1 1/2 lime, juice of
- 1/3 cup Extra Virgin Olive Oil
- Salt and pepper
- 1 tsp ground sumac
- 1/4 tsp ground cinnamon
- scant 1/4 tsp ground allspice

Directions for Cooking:

1) For 5 minutes toast the pita bread in the toaster oven. And then break the pita bread into pieces.
2) In a large pan on medium fire, heat 3 tbsp of olive oil in for 3 minutes. Add pita bread and fry until browned, around 4 minutes while tossing around.
3) Add salt, pepper and 1/2 tsp of sumac. Remove the pita chips from the heat and place on paper towels to drain.
4) Toss well the chopped lettuce, cucumber, tomatoes, green onions, sliced radish, mint leaves and parsley in a large salad bowl.
5) To make the lime vinaigrette, whisk together all ingredients in a small bowl.
6) Drizzle over salad and toss well to coat. Mix in the pita bread.
7) Serve and enjoy.

Nutrition Information:

Calories per Serving: 192; Carbs: 16.1g; Protein: 3.9g; Fats: 13.8g

53

Garlic & Tomato Gluten Free Focaccia

Serves: 8, Cooking Time: 20 minutes

Ingredients:

- 1 egg
- ½ tsp lemon juice
- 1 tbsp honey
- 4 tbsp olive oil
- A pinch of sugar
- 1 ¼ cup warm water
- 1 tbsp active dry yeast
- 2 tsp rosemary, chopped
- 2 tsp thyme, chopped
- 2 tsp basil, chopped
- 2 cloves garlic, minced
- 1 ¼ tsp sea salt
- 2 tsp xanthan gum
- ½ cup millet flour
- 1 cup potato starch, not flour
- 1 cup sorghum flour
- Gluten free cornmeal for dusting

Directions for Cooking:

1) For 5 minutes, turn on the oven and then turn it off, while keeping oven door closed.
2) In a small bowl, mix warm water and pinch of sugar. Add yeast and swirl gently. Leave for 7 minutes.
3) In a large mixing bowl, whisk well herbs, garlic, salt, xanthan gum, starch, and flours.
4) Once yeast is done proofing, pour into bowl of flours. Whisk in egg, lemon juice, honey, and olive oil.
5) Mix thoroughly and place in a well-greased square pan, dusted with cornmeal.
6) Top with fresh garlic, more herbs, and sliced tomatoes.
7) Place in the warmed oven and let it rise for half an hour.
8) Turn on oven to 375oF and after preheating time it for 20 minutes. Focaccia is done once tops are lightly browned.
9) Remove from oven and pan immediately and let it cool.
10) Best served when warm.

Nutrition Information:
Calories per Serving: 251; Carbs: 38.4g; Protein: 5.4g; Fat: 9.0g

Grilled Burgers with Mushrooms

Serves: 4, Cooking Time: 10 minutes

Ingredients:

- 2 Bibb lettuce, halved
- 4 slices red onion
- 4 slices tomato
- 4 whole wheat buns, toasted
- 2 tbsp olive oil
- ¼ tsp cayenne pepper, optional
- 1 garlic clove, minced
- 1 tbsp sugar
- ½ cup water
- 1/3 cup balsamic vinegar
- 4 large Portobello mushroom caps, around 5-inches in diameter

Directions for Cooking:

1) Remove stems from mushrooms and clean with a damp cloth. Transfer into a baking dish with gill-side up.
2) In a bowl, mix thoroughly olive oil, cayenne pepper, garlic, sugar, water and vinegar. Pour over mushrooms and marinate mushrooms in the ref for at least an hour.
3) Once the one hour is nearly up, preheat grill to medium high fire and grease grill grate.
4) Grill mushrooms for five minutes per side or until tender. Baste mushrooms with marinade so it doesn't dry up.
5) To assemble, place ½ of bread bun on a plate, top with a slice of onion, mushroom, tomato and one lettuce leaf. Cover with the other top half of the bun. Repeat process with remaining ingredients, serve and enjoy.

Nutrition Information:

Calories per Serving: 244.1; Carbs: 32g; Protein: 8.1g; Fat: 9.3g

Mediterranean Baba Ghanoush

Serves: 4 , Cooking Time: 25 minutes

Ingredients:

- 1 bulb garlic
- 1 red bell pepper, halved and seeded
- 1 tbsp chopped fresh basil
- 1 tbsp olive oil
- 1 tsp black pepper
- 2 eggplants, sliced lengthwise
- 2 rounds of flatbread or pita
- Juice of 1 lemon

Directions for Cooking:

1) Grease grill grate with cooking spray and preheat grill to medium high.
2) Slice tops of garlic bulb and wrap in foil. Place in the cooler portion of the grill and roast for at least 20 minutes.
3) Place bell pepper and eggplant slices on the hottest part of grill.
4) Grill for at least two to three minutes each side.
5) Once bulbs are done, peel off skins of roasted garlic and place peeled garlic into food processor.
6) Add olive oil, pepper, basil, lemon juice, grilled red bell pepper and grilled eggplant.
7) Puree until smooth and transfer into a bowl.
8) Grill bread at least 30 seconds per side to warm.
9) Serve bread with the pureed dip and enjoy.

Nutrition Information:

Calories per Serving: 213.6; Carbs: 36.3g; Protein: 6.3g; Fat: 4.8g

Multi Grain & Gluten Free Dinner Rolls

Serves: 8, Cooking Time: 20 minutes

Ingredients:

- ½ tsp apple cider vinegar
- 3 tbsp olive oil
- 2 eggs
- 1 tsp baking powder
- 1 tsp salt
- 2 tsp xanthan gum
- ½ cup tapioca starch
- ¼ cup brown teff flour
- ¼ cup flax meal
- ¼ cup amaranth flour
- ¼ cup sorghum flour
- ¾ cup brown rice flour

Directions for Cooking:

1) Mix well water and honey in a small bowl and add yeast. Leave it for exactly 10 minutes.
2) In a large bowl, mix the following with a paddle mixer: baking powder, salt, xanthan gum, flax meal, sorghum flour, teff flour, tapioca starch, amaranth flour, and brown rice flour.
3) In a medium bowl, whisk well vinegar, olive oil, and eggs.
4) Into bowl of dry ingredients pour in vinegar and yeast mixture and mix well.
5) Grease a 12-muffin tin with cooking spray. Transfer dough evenly into 12 muffin tins and leave it for an hour to rise.
6) Then preheat oven to 375oF and bake dinner rolls until tops are golden brown, around 20 minutes.
7) Remove dinner rolls from oven and muffin tins immediately and let it cool.
8) Best served when warm.

Nutrition Information:

Calories per Serving: 207; Carbs: 28.4g; Protein: 4.6g; Fat: 8.3g

Quinoa Pizza Muffins

Serves: 4 , Cooking Time: 30 minutes

Ingredients:

- 1 cup uncooked quinoa
- 2 large eggs
- ½ medium onion, diced
- 1 cup diced bell pepper
- 1 cup shredded mozzarella cheese
- 1 tbsp dried basil
- 1 tbsp dried oregano
- 2 tsp garlic powder
- 1/8 tsp salt
- 1 tsp crushed red peppers
- ½ cup roasted red pepper, chopped*
- Pizza Sauce, about 1-2 cups

Directions for Cooking:

1) Preheat oven to 350oF.
2) Cook quinoa according to directions.
3) Combine all ingredients (except sauce) into bowl. Mix all ingredients well.
4) Scoop quinoa pizza mixture into muffin tin evenly. Makes 12 muffins.
5) Bake for 30 minutes until muffins turn golden in color and the edges are getting crispy.
6) Top with 1 or 2 tbsp pizza sauce and enjoy!

Nutrition Information:

Calories per Serving: 303; Carbs: 41.3g; Protein: 21.0g; Fat: 6.1g

Rosemary-Walnut Loaf Bread

Serves: 8, Cooking Time: 45 minutes

Ingredients:

- ½ cup chopped walnuts
- 4 tbsp fresh, chopped rosemary
- 1 1/3 cups lukewarm carbonated water
- 1 tbsp honey
- ½ cup extra virgin olive oil
- 1 tsp apple cider vinegar
- 3 eggs
- 5 tsp instant dry yeast granules
- 1 tsp salt
- 1 tbsp xanthan gum
- ¼ cup buttermilk powder
- 1 cup white rice flour
- 1 cup tapioca starch
- 1 cup arrowroot starch
- 1 ¼ cups all-purpose Bob's Red Mill gluten-free flour mix

Directions for Cooking:

1) In a large mixing bowl, whisk well eggs. Add 1 cup warm water, honey, olive oil, and vinegar.
2) While beating continuously, add the rest of the ingredients except for rosemary and walnuts.
3) Continue beating. If dough is too stiff, add a bit of warm water. Dough should be shaggy and thick.
4) Then add rosemary and walnuts continue kneading until evenly distributed.
5) Cover bowl of dough with a clean towel, place in a warm spot, and let it rise for 30 minutes.
6) Fifteen minutes into rising time, preheat oven to 400oF.
7) Generously grease with olive oil a 2-quart Dutch oven and preheat inside oven without the lid.
8) Once dough is done rising, remove pot from oven, and place dough inside. With a wet spatula, spread top of dough evenly in pot.
9) Brush tops of bread with 2 tbsp of olive oil, cover Dutch oven and bake for 35 to 45 minutes.

10) Once bread is done, remove from oven. And gently remove bread from pot.

11) Allow bread to cool at least ten minutes before slicing.

12) Serve and enjoy.

Nutrition Information:

Calories per Serving: 424; Carbs: 56.8g; Protein: 7.0g; Fat: 19.0g

Tasty Crabby Panini

Serves: 4 , Cooking Time: 10 minutes

Ingredients:

- 1 tbsp Olive oil
- French bread split and sliced diagonally
- 1 lb. blue crab meat or shrimp or spiny lobster or stone crab
- ½ cup celery
- ¼ cup green onion chopped
- 1 tsp Worcestershire sauce
- 1 tsp lemon juice
- 1 tbsp Dijon mustard
- ½ cup light mayonnaise

Directions for Cooking:

1) In a medium bowl mix the following thoroughly: celery, onion, Worcestershire, lemon juice, mustard and mayonnaise. Season with pepper and salt. Then gently add in the almonds and crabs.
2) Spread olive oil on sliced sides of bread and smear with crab mixture before covering with another bread slice.
3) Grill sandwich in a Panini press until bread is crisped and ridged.

Nutrition Information:

Calories per Serving: 248; Carbs: 12.0g; Protein: 24.5g; Fat: 10.9g

Chapter 6 Salad Recipes

Balela Salad From the Middle East

Serves: 6, Cooking Time: 0 minutes

Salad Ingredients:
- 1 jalapeno, finely chopped (optional)
- 1/2 green bell pepper, cored and chopped
- 2 1/2 cups grape tomatoes, slice in halves
- 1/2 cup sun-dried tomatoes
- 1/2 cup freshly chopped parsley leaves
- 1/2 cup freshly chopped mint or basil leaves
- 1/3 cup pitted Kalamata olives
- 1/4 cup pitted green olives
- 3 1/2 cups cooked chickpeas, drained and rinsed
- 3–5 green onions, both white and green parts, chopped

Dressing Ingredients:
- 1 garlic clove, minced
- 1 tsp ground sumac
- 1/2 tsp Aleppo pepper
- 1/4 cup Early Harvest Greek extra virgin olive oil
- 1/4 to 1/2 tsp crushed red pepper (optional)
- 2 tbsp lemon juice
- 2 tbsp white wine vinegar
- Salt and black pepper, a generous pinch to your taste

Directions for Cooking:
1) mix together the salad ingredients in a large salad bowl.
2) In a separate smaller bowl or jar, mix together the dressing ingredients.
3) Drizzle the dressing over the salad and gently toss to coat.
4) Set aside for 30 minutes to allow the flavors to mix.
5) Serve and enjoy.

Nutrition Information:
Calories per Serving: 257; Carbs: 30.5g; Protein: 8.4g; Fats: 12.6g

Grilled Halloumi Cheese Salad

Serves: 1, Cooking Time: 10 minutes

Ingredients:

- 0.5 oz chopped walnuts
- 1 handful baby arugula
- 1 Persian cucumber, sliced into circles about ½-inch thick
- 3 oz halloumi cheese
- 5 grape tomatoes, sliced in half
- balsamic vinegar
- olive oil
- salt

Directions for Cooking:

1) Into 1/3 slices, cut the cheese. For 3 to 5 minutes each side, grill the kinds of cheese until you can see grill marks.
2) In a salad bowl, add arugula, cucumber, and tomatoes. Drizzle with olive oil and balsamic vinegar. Season with salt and toss well coat.
3) Sprinkle walnuts and add grilled halloumi.
4) Serve and enjoy.

Nutrition Information:

Calories per serving: 543; Protein: 21.0g; Carbs: 9.0g; Fat: 47.0g

Broccoli Salad Moroccan Style

Serves: 4, Cooking Time: 0 minutes

Ingredients:

- ¼ tsp sea salt
- ¼ tsp ground cinnamon
- ½ tsp ground turmeric
- ¾ tsp ground ginger
- ½ tbsp extra virgin olive oil
- ½ tbsp apple cider vinegar
- 2 tbsp chopped green onion
- 1/3 cup coconut cream
- ½ cup carrots, shredded
- 1 small head of broccoli, chopped

Directions for Cooking:

1) In a large salad bowl, mix well salt, cinnamon, turmeric, ginger, olive oil, and vinegar.
2) Add remaining ingredients, tossing well to coat.
3) Pop in the ref for at least 30 to 60 minutes before serving.

Nutrition Information:

Calories per serving: 90.5; Protein: 1.3g; Carbs: 4g; Fat: 7.7g

Garden Salad with Oranges and Olives

Serves: 4 , Cooking Time: 15 minutes

Ingredients:

- ½ cup red wine vinegar
- 1 tbsp extra virgin olive oil
- 1 tbsp finely chopped celery
- 1 tbsp finely chopped red onion
- 16 large ripe black olives
- 2 garlic cloves
- 2 navel oranges, peeled and segmented
- 4 boneless, skinless chicken breasts, 4-oz each
- 4 garlic cloves, minced
- 8 cups leaf lettuce, washed and dried
- Cracked black pepper to taste

Directions for Cooking:

1) Prepare the dressing by mixing pepper, celery, onion, olive oil, garlic and vinegar in a small bowl. Whisk well to combine.
2) Lightly grease grate and preheat grill to high.
3) Rub chicken with the garlic cloves and discard garlic.
4) Grill chicken for 5 minutes per side or until cooked through.
5) Remove from grill and let it stand for 5 minutes before cutting into ½-inch strips.
6) In 4 serving plates, evenly arrange two cups lettuce, ¼ of the sliced oranges and 4 olives per plate.
7) Top each plate with ¼ serving of grilled chicken, evenly drizzle with dressing, serve and enjoy.

Nutrition Information:

Calories per serving: 259.8; Protein: 48.9g; Carbs: 12.9g; Fat: 1.4g

Lemony Lentil Salad with Salmon

Serves: 6, Cooking Time: 0 minutes

Ingredients:

- ¼ tsp salt
- ½ cup chopped red onion
- 1 cup diced seedless cucumber
- 1 medium red bell pepper, diced
- 1/3 cup extra virgin olive oil
- 1/3 cup fresh dill, chopped
- 1/3 cup lemon juice
- 2 15oz cans of lentils
- 2 7oz cans of salmon, drained and flaked
- 2 tsp Dijon mustard
- Pepper to taste

Directions for Cooking:

1) In a bowl, mix together, lemon juice, mustard, dill, salt and pepper.
2) Gradually add the oil, bell pepper, onion, cucumber, salmon flakes and lentils.
3) Toss to coat evenly.

Nutrition Information:

Calories per serving: 349.1; Protein: 27.1g; Carbs: 35.2g; Fat: 11.1g

Mozzarella and Fig Salad

Serves: 4 , Cook Time: 3 minutes

Ingredients:

- 0.10 lbs of toasted and chopped hazelnut
- 0.45 lb of trimmed green beans
- ¼ lb mozzarella, ripped into chunks
- 1 shallot, sliced thinly
- 1 tbsp fig jam or relish
- 3 tbsp balsamic vinegar
- 3 tbsp extra virgin olive oil
- 6 small figs, quartered
- Small handful of basil leaves, torn

Directions for Cooking:

1) For two to three minutes, blanch beans in salted water. Then remove the water, wash with cold tap water, drain and let dry on top of kitchen towel.
2) Once the beans are dried, place on a food platter and add basil, hazelnuts, mozzarella, shallots and figs.
3) To create dressing, use a medium lidded jar and add your choice of seasoning, olive oil, fig jam and vinegar. Cover the jar and shake vigorously before pouring over the salad.

Nutrition Information:

Calories per Serving: 294.8; Fat: 17.6g; Protein: 12.7g; Carbs: 21.4g

Raw Winter Persimmon Salad

Serves: 2 , Cook Time: 0 minutes

Ingredients:

- ½ cup coarsely chopped pistachio
- ½ cup sweet potato, spiralized
- 1 red bell pepper, diced
- 1 red bell pepper, julienned
- 1 ripe fuyu persimmon, diced
- 1 tbsp chili powder
- 2 fuyu persimmon, sliced
- 3 tbsp lime juice
- 4 cups mixed greens
- a pinch of chipotle powder
- salt to taste

Directions for Cooking:

1) In a salad bowl, mix and arrange persimmons, bell pepper and sweet potatoes. Set aside.
2) In a food processor, puree salt, lime juice, chipotle powder, chili powder, diced persimmon and diced bell pepper until smooth and creamy.
3) Pour over salad, toss to mix.
4) Serve and enjoy.

Nutrition Information:

Calories per Serving: 467.4; Fat: 15.4g; Protein: 11.3g; Carbs: 70.9g

Tabbouleh- Arabian Salad

Serves: 6 , Cook Time: 0 minutes

Ingredients:

- ¼ cup chopped fresh mint
- 1 2/3 cups boiling water
- 1 cucumber, peeled, seeded and chopped
- 1 cup bulgur
- 1 cup chopped fresh parsley
- 1 cup chopped green onions
- 1 tsp salt
- 1/3 cup lemon juice
- 1/3 cup olive oil
- 3 tomatoes, chopped
- Ground black pepper to taste

Directions for Cooking:

1) In a large bowl, mix together boiling water and bulgur. Let soak and set aside for an hour while covered.
2) After one hour, toss in cucumber, tomatoes, mint, parsley, onions, lemon juice and oil. Then season with black pepper and salt to taste. Toss well and refrigerate for another hour while covered before serving.

Nutrition Information:

Calories per serving: 185.5; Fat: 13.1g; Protein: 4.1g; Carbs: 12.8g

Chapter 7 Beans Recipes

Bean and Toasted Pita Salad

Serves: 4, Cooking Time: 10 minutes

Ingredients:

- 3 tbsp chopped fresh mint
- 3 tbsp chopped fresh parsley
- 1 cup crumbled feta cheese
- 1 cup sliced romaine lettuce
- ½ cucumber, peeled and sliced
- 1 cup diced plum tomatoes
- 2 cups cooked pinto beans, well drained and slightly warmed
- Pepper to taste
- 3 tbsp extra virgin olive oil
- 2 tbsp ground toasted cumin seeds
- 2 tbsp fresh lemon juice
- 1/8 tsp salt
- 2 cloves garlic, peeled
- 2 6-inch whole wheat pita bread, cut or torn into bite-sized pieces

Directions for Cooking:

1) In large baking sheet, spread torn pita bread and bake in a preheated 400oF oven for 6 minutes.
2) With the back of a knife, mash garlic and salt until paste like. Add into a medium bowl.
3) Whisk in ground cumin and lemon juice. In a steady and slow stream, pour oil as you whisk continuously. Season with pepper.
4) In a large salad bowl, mix cucumber, tomatoes and beans. Pour in dressing, toss to coat well.
5) Add mint, parsley, feta, lettuce and toasted pita, toss to mix once again and serve.

Nutrition Information:

Calories per serving: 427; Protein: 17.7g; Carbs: 47.3g; Fat: 20.4g

Beans and Spinach Mediterranean Salad

Serves: 4, Cooking Time: 30 minutes

Ingredients:

- 1 can (14 ounces) water-packed artichoke hearts, rinsed, drained and quartered
- 1 can (14-1/2 ounces) no-salt-added diced tomatoes, undrained
- 1 can (15 ounces) cannellini beans, rinsed and drained
- 1 small onion, chopped
- 1 tablespoon olive oil
- 1/4 teaspoon pepper
- 1/4 teaspoon salt
- 1/8 teaspoon crushed red pepper flakes
- 2 garlic cloves, minced
- 2 tablespoons Worcestershire sauce
- 6 ounces fresh baby spinach (about 8 cups)
- Additional olive oil, optional

Directions for Cooking:

1) Place a saucepan on medium high fire and heat for a minute.
2) Add oil and heat for 2 minutes. Stir in onion and sauté for 4 minutes. Add garlic and sauté for another minute.
3) Stir in seasonings, Worcestershire sauce, and tomatoes. Cook for 5 minutes while stirring continuously until sauce is reduced.
4) Stir in spinach, artichoke hearts, and beans. Sauté for 3 minutes until spinach is wilted and other ingredients are heated through.
5) Serve and enjoy.

Nutrition Information:

Calories per serving: 187; Protein: 8.0g; Carbs: 30.0g; Fat: 4.0g

Chickpea Fried Eggplant Salad

Serves: 4, Cooking Time: 10 minutes

Ingredients:

- 1 cup chopped dill
- 1 cup chopped parsley
- 1 cup cooked or canned chickpeas, drained
- 1 large eggplant, thinly sliced (no more than 1/4 inch in thickness)
- 1 small red onion, sliced in 1/2 moons
- 1/2 English cucumber, diced
- 3 Roma tomatoes, diced
- 3 tbsp Za'atar spice, divided
- oil for frying, preferably extra virgin olive oil
- Salt

Garlic Vinaigrette Ingredients:

- 1 large lime, juice of
- 1/3 cup extra virgin olive oil
- 1–2 garlic cloves, minced
- Salt & Pepper to taste

Directions for Cooking:

1) On a baking sheet, spread out sliced eggplant and season with salt generously. Let it sit for 30 minutes. Then pat dry with paper towel.
2) Place a small pot on medium high fire and fill halfway with oil. Heat oil for 5 minutes. Fry eggplant in batches until golden brown, around 3 minutes per side. Place cooked eggplants on a paper towel lined plate.
3) Once eggplants have cooled, assemble the eggplant on a serving dish. Sprinkle with 1 tbsp of Za'atar.
4) Mix dill, parsley, red onions, chickpeas, cucumbers, and tomatoes in a large salad bowl. Sprinkle remaining Za'atar and gently toss to mix.
5) Whisk well the vinaigrette ingredients in a small bowl. Drizzle 2 tbsp of the dressing over the fried eggplant. Add remaining dressing over the chickpea salad and mix.
6) Add the chickpea salad to the serving dish with the fried eggplant.
7) Serve and enjoy.

Nutrition Information:

Calories per serving: 642; Protein: 16.6g; Carbs: 25.9g; Fat: 44.0g

Chorizo-Kidney Beans Quinoa Pilaf

Serves: 4, Cooking Time: 35 minutes

Ingredients:

- ¼ pound dried Spanish chorizo diced (about 2/3 cup)
- ¼ teaspoon red pepper flakes
- ¼ teaspoon smoked paprika
- ½ teaspoon cumin
- ½ teaspoon sea salt
- 1 3/4 cups water
- 1 cup quinoa
- 1 large clove garlic minced
- 1 small red bell pepper finely diced
- 1 small red onion finely diced
- 1 tablespoon tomato paste
- 1 15-ounce can kidney beans rinsed and drained

Directions for Cooking:

1) Place a nonstick pot on medium high fire and heat for 2 minutes. Add chorizo and sauté for 5 minutes until lightly browned.
2) Stir in peppers and onion. Sauté for 5 minutes.
3) Add tomato paste, red pepper flakes, salt, paprika, cumin, and garlic. Sauté for 2 minutes.
4) Stir in quinoa and mix well. Sauté for 2 minutes.
5) Add water and beans. Mix well. Cover and simmer for 20 minutes or until liquid is fully absorbed.
6) Turn off fire and fluff quinoa. Let it sit for 5 minutes more while uncovered.
7) Serve and enjoy.

Nutrition Information:

Calories per serving: 260; Protein: 9.6g; Carbs: 40.9g; Fat: 6.8g

Goat Cheese 'n Red Beans Salad

Serves: 6, Cooking Time: 0 minutes

Ingredients:

- 2 cans of Red Kidney Beans, drained and rinsed well
- Water or vegetable broth to cover beans
- 1 bunch parsley, chopped
- 1 1/2 cups red grape tomatoes, halved
- 3 cloves garlic, minced
- 3 tablespoons olive oil
- 3 tablespoons lemon juice
- 1/2 teaspoon salt
- 1/2 teaspoon white pepper
- 6 ounces goat cheese, crumbled

Directions for Cooking:

1) In a large bowl, combine beans, parsley, tomatoes and garlic.
2) Add olive oil, lemon juice, salt and pepper.
3) Mix well and refrigerate until ready to serve.
4) Spoon into individual dishes topped with crumbled goat cheese.

Nutrition Information:

Calories per serving: 385; Protein: 22.5g; Carbs: 44.0g; Fat: 15.0g

Greek Farro Salad

Serves: 4, Cooking Time: 15 minutes

Farro Ingredients:

- ½ teaspoon fine-grain sea salt
- 1 cup farro, rinsed
- 1 tablespoon olive oil
- 2 garlic cloves, pressed or minced

Salad Ingredients:

- ½ small red onion, chopped and then rinsed under water to mellow the flavor
- 1 avocado, sliced into strips
- 1 cucumber, sliced into thin rounds
- 15 pitted Kalamata olives, sliced into rounds
- 1-pint cherry tomatoes, sliced into rounds
- 2 cups cooked chickpeas (or one 14-ounce can, rinsed and drained)
- 5 ounces mixed greens
- Lemon wedges

Herbed Yogurt Ingredients:

- ⅛ teaspoon salt
- 1 ¼ cups plain Greek yogurt
- 1 ½ tablespoon lightly packed fresh dill, roughly chopped
- 1 ½ tablespoon lightly packed fresh mint, torn into pieces
- 1 tablespoon lemon juice (about ½ lemon)
- 1 tablespoon olive oil

Directions for Cooking:

1) In a blender, blend and puree all herbed yogurt ingredients and set aside.
2) Then cook the farro by placing in a pot filled halfway with water. Bring to a boil, reduce fire to a simmer and cook for 15 minutes or until farro is tender. Drain well. Mix in salt, garlic, and olive oil and fluff to coat.
3) Evenly divide the cooled farro into 4 bowls. Evenly divide the salad ingredients on the 4 farro bowl. Top with ¼ of the yogurt dressing.
4) Serve and enjoy.

Nutrition Information:

Calories per serving: 428; Protein: 17.7g; Carbs: 47.6g; Fat: 24.5g

White Bean and Tuna Salad

Serves: 4, Cooking Time: 8 minutes

Ingredients:

- 1 (12 ounce) can solid white albacore tuna, drained
- 1 (16 ounce) can Great Northern beans, drained and rinsed
- 1 (2.25 ounce) can sliced black olives, drained
- 1 teaspoon dried oregano
- 1/2 teaspoon finely grated lemon zest
- 1/4 medium red onion, thinly sliced
- 3 tablespoons lemon juice
- 3/4-pound green beans, trimmed and snapped in half
- 4 large hard-cooked eggs, peeled and quartered
- 6 tablespoons extra-virgin olive oil
- Salt and ground black pepper, to taste

Directions for Cooking:

1) Place a saucepan on medium high fire. Add a cup of water and the green beans. Cover and cook for 8 minutes. Drain immediately once tender.
2) In a salad bowl, whisk well oregano, olive oil, lemon juice, and lemon zest. Season generously with pepper and salt and mix until salt is dissolved.
3) Stir in drained green beans, tuna, beans, olives, and red onion. Mix thoroughly to coat.
4) Adjust seasoning to taste.
5) Spread eggs on top.
6) Serve and enjoy.

Nutrition Information:

Calories per serving: 551; Protein: 36.3g; Carbs: 33.4g; Fat: 30.3g

Spicy Sweet Red Hummus

Serves: 8, Cooking Time: 0 minutes

Ingredients:

- 1 (15 ounce) can garbanzo beans, drained
- 1 (4 ounce) jar roasted red peppers
- 1 1/2 tablespoons tahini
- 1 clove garlic, minced
- 1 tablespoon chopped fresh parsley
- 1/2 teaspoon cayenne pepper
- 1/2 teaspoon ground cumin
- 1/4 teaspoon salt
- 3 tablespoons lemon juice

Directions for Cooking:

1) In a blender, add all ingredients and process until smooth and creamy.
2) Adjust seasoning to taste if needed.
3) Can be stored in an airtight container for up to 5 days.

Nutrition Information:

Calories per serving: 64; Protein: 2.5g; Carbs: 9.6g; Fat: 2.2g

Chapter 8 Seafood Recipes

Berries and Grilled Calamari

Serves: 4, Cook Time: 5 minutes

Ingredients:

- ¼ cup dried cranberries
- ¼ cup extra virgin olive oil
- ¼ cup olive oil
- ¼ cup sliced almonds
- ½ lemon, juiced
- ¾ cup blueberries
- 1 ½ pounds calamari tube, cleaned
- 1 granny smith apple, sliced thinly
- 1 tablespoon fresh lemon juice
- 2 tablespoons apple cider vinegar
- 6 cups fresh spinach
- Freshly grated pepper to taste
- Sea salt to taste

Directions for Cooking:

1) In a small bowl, make the vinaigrette by mixing well the tablespoon of lemon juice, apple cider vinegar, and extra virgin olive oil. Season with pepper and salt to taste. Set aside.
2) Turn on the grill to medium fire and let the grates heat up for a minute or two.
3) In a large bowl, add olive oil and the calamari tube. Season calamari generously with pepper and salt.
4) Place seasoned and oiled calamari onto heated grate and grill until cooked or opaque. This is around two minutes per side.
5) As you wait for the calamari to cook, you can combine almonds, cranberries, blueberries, spinach, and the thinly sliced apple in a large salad bowl. Toss to mix.
6) Remove cooked calamari from grill and transfer on a chopping board. Cut into ¼-inch thick rings and throw into the salad bowl.
7) Drizzle with vinaigrette and toss well to coat salad.
8) Serve and enjoy!

Nutrition Information:

Calories per Serving: 567; Fat: 24.5g; Protein: 54.8g; Carbs: 30.6g

Cajun Garlic Shrimp Noodle Bowl

Serves: 2, Cook Time: 15 minutes

Ingredients:

- ½ teaspoon salt
- 1 onion, sliced
- 1 red pepper, sliced
- 1 tablespoon butter
- 1 teaspoon garlic granules
- 1 teaspoon onion powder
- 1 teaspoon paprika
- 2 large zucchinis, cut into noodle strips
- 20 jumbo shrimps, shells removed and deveined
- 3 cloves garlic, minced
- 3 tablespoon ghee
- A dash of cayenne pepper
- A dash of red pepper flakes

Directions for Cooking:

1) Prepare the Cajun seasoning by mixing the onion powder, garlic granules, pepper flakes, cayenne pepper, paprika and salt. Toss in the shrimp to coat in the seasoning.
2) In a skillet, heat the ghee and sauté the garlic. Add in the red pepper and onions and continue sautéing for 4 minutes.
3) Add the Cajun shrimp and cook until opaque. Set aside.
4) In another pan, heat the butter and sauté the zucchini noodles for three minutes.
5) Assemble by the placing the Cajun shrimps on top of the zucchini noodles.

Nutrition Information:

Calories per Serving: 712; Fat: 30.0g; Protein: 97.8g; Carbs: 20.2g

Creamy Bacon-fish Chowder

Serves: 8, Cooking Time: 30 minutes

Ingredients:

- 1 1/2 lbs. cod
- 1 1/2 tsp dried thyme
- 1 large onion, chopped
- 1 medium carrot, coarsely chopped
- 1 tbsp butter, cut into small pieces
- 1 tsp salt, divided
- 3 1/2 cups baking potato, peeled and cubed
- 3 slices uncooked bacon
- 3/4 tsp freshly ground black pepper, divided
- 4 1/2 cups water
- 4 bay leaves
- 4 cups 2% reduced-fat milk

Directions for Cooking:

1) In a large skillet, add the water and bay leaves and let it simmer. Add the fish. Cover and let it simmer some more until the flesh flakes easily with fork. Remove the fish from the skillet and cut into large pieces. Set aside the cooking liquid.
2) Place Dutch oven in medium heat and cook the bacon until crisp. Remove the bacon and reserve the bacon drippings. Crush the bacon and set aside.
3) Stir potato, onion and carrot in the pan with the bacon drippings, cook over medium heat for 10 minutes. Add the cooking liquid, bay leaves, 1/2 tsp salt, 1/4 tsp pepper and thyme, let it boil. Lower the heat and let simmer for 10 minutes. Add the milk and butter, simmer until the potatoes becomes tender, but do not boil. Add the fish, 1/2 tsp salt, 1/2 tsp pepper. Remove the bay leaves.
4) Serve sprinkled with the crushed bacon.

Nutrition Information:

Calories per serving: 400; Carbs: 34.5g; Protein: 20.8g; Fat: 19.7g

Cucumber-basil Salsa on Halibut Pouches

Serves: 4, Cook Time: 17 minutes

Ingredients:

- 1 lime, thinly sliced into 8 pieces
- 2 cups mustard greens, stems removed
- 2 tsp olive oil
- 4 – 5 radishes trimmed and quartered
- 4 4-oz skinless halibut filets
- 4 large fresh basil leaves
- Cayenne pepper to taste – optional
- Pepper and salt to taste

Salsa Ingredients:

- 1 ½ cups diced cucumber
- 1 ½ finely chopped fresh basil leaves
- 2 tsp fresh lime juice
- Pepper and salt to taste

Directions for Cooking:

1) Preheat oven to 400oF.
2) Prepare parchment papers by making 4 pieces of 15 x 12-inch rectangles. Lengthwise, fold in half and unfold pieces on the table.
3) Season halibut fillets with pepper, salt and cayenne—if using cayenne.
4) Just to the right of the fold going lengthwise, place ½ cup of mustard greens. Add a basil leaf on center of mustard greens and topped with 1 lime slice. Around the greens, layer ¼ of the radishes. Drizzle with ½ tsp of oil, season with pepper and salt. Top it with a slice of halibut fillet.
5) Just as you would make a calzone, fold parchment paper over your filling and crimp the edges of the parchment paper beginning from one end to the other end. To seal the end of the crimped parchment paper, pinch it.
6) Repeat process to remaining ingredients until you have 4 pieces of parchment papers filled with halibut and greens.
7) Place pouches in a baking pan and bake in the oven until halibut is flaky, around 15 to 17 minutes.
8) While waiting for halibut pouches to cook, make your salsa by mixing all salsa ingredients in a medium bowl.

9) Once halibut is cooked, remove from oven and make a tear on top. Be careful of the steam as it is very hot. Equally divide salsa and spoon ¼ of salsa on top of halibut through the slit you have created.

10) Serve and enjoy.

Nutrition Information:

Calories per serving: 335.4; Protein: 20.2g; Fat: 16.3g; Carbs: 22.1g

Dill Relish on White Sea Bass

Serves: 4 , Cook Time: 12 minutes

Ingredients:

- 1 ½ tbsp chopped white onion
- 1 ½ tsp chopped fresh dill
- 1 lemon, quartered
- 1 tsp Dijon mustard
- 1 tsp lemon juice
- 1 tsp pickled baby capers, drained
- 4 pieces of 4-oz white sea bass fillets

Directions for Cooking:

1) Preheat oven to 375oF.
2) Mix lemon juice, mustard, dill, capers and onions in a small bowl.
3) Prepare four aluminum foil squares and place 1 fillet per foil.
4) Squeeze a lemon wedge per fish.
5) Evenly divide into 4 the dill spread and drizzle over fillet.
6) Close the foil over the fish securely and pop in the oven.
7) Bake for 10 to 12 minutes or until fish is cooked through.
8) Remove from foil and transfer to a serving platter, serve and enjoy.

Nutrition Information:

Calories per serving: 115; Protein: 7g; Fat: 1g; Carbs: 12g

Chapter 9 Poultry and Meat Recipes

Vegetable Lover's Chicken Soup

Serves: 4, Cooking Time: 20 minutes

Ingredients:

- 1 ½ cups baby spinach
- 2 tbsp orzo (tiny pasta)
- ¼ cup dry white wine
- 1 14oz low sodium chicken broth
- 2 plum tomatoes, chopped
- 1/8 tsp salt
- ½ tsp Italian seasoning
- 1 large shallot, chopped
- 1 small zucchini, diced
- 8-oz chicken tenders
- 1 tbsp extra virgin olive oil

Directions for Cooking:

1) In a large saucepan, heat oil over medium heat and add the chicken. Stir occasionally for 8 minutes until browned. Transfer in a plate. Set aside.
2) In the same saucepan, add the zucchini, Italian seasoning, shallot and salt and stir often until the vegetables are softened, around 4 minutes.
3) Add the tomatoes, wine, broth and orzo and increase the heat to high to bring the mixture to boil. Reduce the heat and simmer.
4) Add the cooked chicken and stir in the spinach last.
5) Serve hot.

Nutrition Information:

Calories per Serving: 207; Carbs: 14.8g; Protein: 12.2g; Fat: 11.4g

Stewed Chicken Greek Style

Servers: 10, Cook Time: 1 hour and 15 minutes

Ingredients:

- ½ cup red wine
- 1 ½ cups chicken stock or more if needed
- 1 cup olive oil
- 1 cup tomato sauce
- 1 pc, 4lbs whole chicken cut into pieces
- 1 pinch dried oregano or to taste
- 10 small shallots, peeled
- 2 bay leaves
- 2 cloves garlic, finely chopped
- 2 tbsp chopped fresh parsley
- 2 tsps butter
- Salt and ground black pepper to taste

Directions for Cooking:

1) Bring to a boil a large pot of lightly salted water. Mix in the shallots and let boil uncovered until tender for around three minutes. Then drain the shallots and dip in cold water until no longer warm.

2) In another large pot over medium fire, heat butter and olive oil until bubbling and melted. Then sauté in the chicken and shallots for 15 minutes or until chicken is cooked and shallots are soft and translucent. Then add the chopped garlic and cook for three mins more.

3) Then add bay leaves, oregano, salt and pepper, parsley, tomato sauce and the red wine and let simmer for a minute before adding the chicken stock. Stir before covering and let cook for 50 minutes on medium-low fire or until chicken is tender.

Nutrition Information:

Calories per Serving: 644.8; Carbs: 8.2g; Protein: 62.1g; Fat: 40.4g

Peas and Ham Thick Soup

Serves: 4, Cooking Time: 30 minutes

Ingredients:

- Pepper and salt to taste
- 1 lb. ham, coarsely chopped
- 24 oz frozen sweet peas
- 4 cup ham stock
- ¼ cup white wine
- 1 carrot, chopped coarsely
- 1 onion, chopped coarsely
- 2 tbsp butter, divided

Directions for Cooking:

1) On medium fireplace a medium pot and heat oil. Sauté for 6 minutes the onion or until soft and translucent.
2) Add wine and cook for 4 minutes or until nearly evaporated.
3) Add ham stock and bring to a simmer and simmer continuously while covered for 4 minutes.
4) Add peas and cook for 7 minutes or until tender.
5) Meanwhile, in a nonstick fry pan, cook to a browned crisp the ham in 1 tbsp butter, around 6 minutes. Remove from fire and set aside.
6) When peas are soft, transfer to a blender and puree. Return to pot, continue cooking while seasoning with pepper, salt and ½ of crisped ham. Once soup is to your desired taste, turn off fire.
7) Transfer to 4 serving bowls and garnish evenly with crisped ham.

Nutrition Information:

Calories per Serving: 403; Carbs: 32.5g; Protein: 37.3g; Fat: 12.5g

Mustard Chops with Apricot-basil Relish

Serves: 4, Cooking Time: 12 minutes

Ingredients:

- ¼ cup basil, finely shredded
- ¼ cup olive oil
- ½ cup mustard
- ¾ lb. fresh apricots, stone removed, and fruit diced
- 1 shallot, diced small
- 1 tsp ground cardamom
- 3 tbsp raspberry vinegar
- 4 pork chops
- Pepper and salt

Directions for Cooking:

1) Make sure that pork chops are defrosted well. Season with pepper and salt. Slather both sides of each pork chop with mustard. Preheat grill to medium-high fire.
2) In a medium bowl, mix cardamom, olive oil, vinegar, basil, shallot, and apricots. Toss to combine and season with pepper and salt, mixing once again.
3) Grill chops for 5 to 6 minutes per side. As you flip, baste with mustard.
4) Serve pork chops with the Apricot-Basil relish and enjoy.

Nutrition Information:

Calories per Serving: 486.5; Carbs: 7.3g; Protein: 42.1g; Fat: 32.1g

Meatball Gyro Pita Sandwich

Serves: 4, Cooking Time: 30 minutes

Ingredients:

- 1 cup Greek yogurt
- 1/4 cup cucumber, grated
- 4 teaspoons minced garlic, divided
- 1 teaspoon extra-virgin olive oil
- 1 tablespoon fresh dill
- 1 teaspoon sea salt, divided and more to taste
- 1/2 teaspoon cracked black pepper, divided and more to taste
- 1 tablespoon fresh lemon juice
- 1-pound ground chuck
- 1/4 cup Italian breadcrumbs
- 1 large egg
- 3 tablespoons chopped flat leaf Italian parsley, divided
- 1/2 teaspoon ground cumin
- 1 cup cucumbers, diced finely
- 1 cup finely diced tomatoes
- 1/2 cup finely diced red onion
- 4 flatbreads

Directions for Cooking:

1) First make the tzatziki sauce by combining ¼ tsp pepper, ½ tsp salt, 1 tbsp fresh dill, 1 tsp olive oil, 1 tsp minced garlic, ¼ cup grated cucumber, 1 tbsp fresh lemon juice, and 1 cup Greek yogurt. Mix well in a Ball jar, adjust seasoning to taste if needed, cover, and refrigerate until ready to use. Best when made at least a day ahead.
2) Preheat the oven to 425°F.
3) In a large mixing bowl, combine 1-pound ground chuck, 1/4 cup dry Italian breadcrumbs, 1 large egg, 2 tablespoons chopped fresh flat-leaf Italian parsley, 1 tablespoon freshly minced garlic, 1/2 teaspoon ground cumin, 1/2 teaspoon sea salt, and 1/4 teaspoon freshly cracked black pepper.
4) Mix well to combine and then form into 16 equal sized meatballs.
5) Place meatballs on a lightly greased baking sheet and bake in the pre-heated oven for 16 minutes or until cooked through and no longer pink inside. When done, remove from oven and let it rest for 5 minutes.

6) While the meatballs are cooking, mix well a tbsp of parsley, red onions, tomatoes, and cucumbers in a bowl. Season with pepper and salt.

7) Toast flatbread in toaster oven for 5 minutes.

8) To assemble, place about 4 meatballs down the center of each flatbread. Spoon a generous amount of Tzatziki sauce on the center next to the meatballs and top with a heaping spoonful of the tomato-cucumber salad. Wrap up and enjoy!

Nutrition Information:

Calories per Serving: 540; Carbs: 51.0g; Protein: 33.0g; Fats: 22.0g

Chapter 10 Fruits and Sweets Recipes

Blueberry Frozen Yogurt

Serves: 6, Cooking Time: 30 minutes

Ingredients:

- 1-pint blueberries, fresh
- 2/3 cup honey
- 1 small lemon, juiced and zested
- 2 cups yogurt, chilled

Directions for Cooking:

1) In a saucepan, combine the blueberries, honey, lemon juice, and zest.
2) Heat over medium heat and allow to simmer for 15 minutes while stirring constantly.
3) Once the liquid has reduced, transfer the fruits in a bowl and allow to cool in the fridge for another 15 minutes.
4) Once chilled, mix together with the chilled yogurt.

Nutrition Information:

Calories per serving: 233; Carbs:52.2 g; Protein:3.5 g; Fat: 2.9g

Delectable Strawberry Popsicle

Serves: 5, Cooking Time: 10 minutes

Ingredients:

- 2 ½ cups fresh strawberry
- ½ cup almond milk

Directions for Cooking:

1) Blend all ingredients until smooth.
2) Pour into the popsicle molds with sticks and freeze for at least 4 hours.
3) Serve chilled.

Nutrition Information:

Calories per serving: 35; Carbs: 7.7g; Protein: 0.6g; Fat:0.5 g

Deliciously Cold Lychee Sorbet

Serves: 4, Cooking Time: 5 minutes

Ingredients:

- 2 cups fresh lychees, pitted and sliced
- 2 tablespoons honey
- Mint leaves for garnish

Directions for Cooking:

1) Place the lychee slices and honey in a food processor.
2) Pulse until smooth.
3) Pour in a container and place inside the fridge for at least two hours.
4) Scoop the sorbet and serve with mint leaves.

Nutrition Information:

Calories per serving: 151; Carbs: 38.9g; Protein: 0.7g; Fat: 0.4

Easy Fruit Compote

Serves: 2, Cooking Time: 15 minutes

Ingredients:

- 1-pound fresh fruits of your choice
- 2 tablespoons maple syrup
- A dash of salt

Directions for Cooking:

1) Slice the fruits thinly and place them in a saucepan.
2) Add the honey and salt.
3) Heat the saucepan over medium low heat and allow the fruits to simmer for 15 minutes or until the liquid has reduced.
4) Make sure that you stir constantly to prevent the fruits from sticking at the bottom of your pan and eventually burning.
5) Transfer in a lidded jar.
6) Allow to cool.
7) Serve with slices of whole wheat bread or vegan ice cream.

Nutrition Information:

Calories per serving:218; Carbs: 56.8g; Protein: 0.9g; Fat: 0.2g

Five Berry Mint Orange Infusion

Serves: 12, Cooking Time: 10 minutes

Ingredients:

- ½ cup water
- 3 orange pekoe tea bags
- 3 sprigs of mint
- 1 cup fresh strawberries
- 1 cup fresh golden raspberries
- 1 cup fresh raspberries
- 1 cup blackberries
- 1 cup fresh blueberries
- 1 cup pitted fresh cherries
- 1 bottle Sauvignon Blanc
- ½ cup pomegranate juice, natural
- 1 teaspoon vanilla

Directions for Cooking:

1) In a saucepan, bring water to a boil over medium heat. Add the tea bags, mint and stir. Let it stand for 10 minutes.
2) In a large bowl, combine the rest of the ingredients.
3) Put in the fridge to chill for at least 3 hours.

Nutrition Information:

Calories per serving: 140; Carbs: 32.1g; Protein: 1.2g; Fat: 1.5g

Greek Yogurt Muesli Parfaits

Serves: 4, Cooking Time: 10 minutes

Ingredients:

- 4 cups Greek yogurt
- 1 cup whole wheat muesli
- 2 cups fresh berries of your choice

Directions for Cooking:

1) Layer the four glasses with Greek yogurt at the bottom, muesli on top, and berries.
2) Repeat the layers until the glass is full.
3) Place in the fridge for at least 2 hours to chill.

Nutrition Information:

Calories per serving: 280; Carbs: 36g; Protein:23 g; Fat: 4g

Mediterranean Baked Apples

Serves: 4, Cooking Time: 25 minutes

Ingredients:

- 1.5 pounds apples, peeled and sliced
- Juice from ½ lemon
- A dash of cinnamon

Directions for Cooking:

1) Preheat the oven to 2500F.
2) Line a baking sheet with parchment paper then set aside.
3) In a medium bowl, apples with lemon juice and cinnamon.
4) Place the apples on the parchment paper-lined baking sheet.
5) Bake for 25 minutes until crisp.

Nutrition Information:

Calories per serving: 90; Carbs: 23.9g; Protein: 0.5g; Fat: 0.3g

Appendix: 21 Days Meal Plan

Meal Plan	Breakfast	Lunch	Dinner	Snacks
Day-1	Breakfast Egg on Avocado	Berries and Grilled Calamari	Balela Salad from the Middle East	Blueberry Frozen Yogurt
Day-2	Breakfast Egg-Artichoke Casserole	Cajun Garlic Shrimp Noodle Bowl	Grilled Halloumi Cheese Salad	Delectable Strawberry Popsicle
Day-3	Brekky Egg-Potato Hash	Creamy Bacon-Fish Chowder	Broccoli Salad Moroccan Style	Deliciously Cold Lychee Sorbet
Day-4	Dill and Tomato Frittata	Cucumber-Basil Salsa on Halibut Pouches	Garden Salad with Oranges and Olives	Easy Fruit Compote
Day-5	Paleo Almond Banana Pancakes	Dill Relish on White Sea Bass	Lemony Lentil Salad with Salmon	Five Berry Mint Orange Infusion
Day-6	Banana-Coconut Breakfast	Vegetable Lover's Chicken Soup	Mozzarella and Fig Salad	Greek Yogurt Muesli Parfaits
Day-7	Basil and Tomato Soup	Stewed Chicken Greek Style	Raw Winter Persimmon Salad	Mediterranean Baked Apples
Day-8	Butternut Squash Hummus	Peas and Ham Thick Soup	Tabbouleh-Arabian Salad	Butternut Squash Hummus
Day-9	Cajun Jambalaya Soup	Mustard Chops with Apricot-Basil Relish	Bean and Toasted Pita Salad	Amazingly Good Parsley Tabbouleh
Day-10	Collard Green Wrap Greek Style	Meatball Gyro Pita Sandwich	Beans and Spinach Mediterranean Salad	Appetizing Mushroom Lasagna
Day-11	Portobello Mushroom Pizza	Avocado and Turkey Mix Panini	Chickpea Fried Eggplant Salad	Artichokes, Olives & Tuna Pasta
Day-12	Roasted Root Veggies	Cucumber, Chicken and Mango Wrap	Chorizo-Kidney Beans Quinoa Pilaf	Blueberry Frozen Yogurt

Day-13	Amazingly Good Parsley Tabbouleh	Fattoush Salad – Middle East Bread Salad	Goat Cheese 'n Red Beans Salad	Easy Fruit Compote
Day-14	Appetizing Mushroom Lasagna	Garlic & Tomato Gluten Free Focaccia	Greek Farro Salad	Grilled Halloumi Cheese Salad
Day-15	Artichokes, Olives & Tuna Pasta	Grilled Burgers with Mushrooms	White Bean and Tuna Salad	Deliciously Cold Lychee Sorbet
Day-16	Balela Salad from the Middle East	Mediterranean Baba Ghanoush	Spicy Sweet Red Hummus	Greek Farro Salad
Day-17	Grilled Halloumi Cheese Salad	Multi Grain & Gluten Free Dinner Rolls	Tasty Lasagna Rolls	Five Berry Mint Orange Infusion
Day-18	Broccoli Salad Moroccan Style	Quinoa Pizza Muffins	Tortellini Salad with Broccoli	Greek Yogurt Muesli Parfaits
Day-19	Mozzarella and Fig Salad	Rosemary-Walnut Loaf Bread	Simple Penne Anti-Pasto	Easy Fruit Compote
Day-20	Tabbouleh-Arabian Salad	asty Crabby Panini	Red Quinoa Peach Porridge	Delectable Strawberry Popsicle
Day-21	Greek Farro Salad	Creamy Bacon-Fish Chowder	Bell Peppers 'n Tomato-Chickpea Rice	Blueberry Frozen Yogurt

Made in the USA
Coppell, TX
03 May 2020